THE KEY TO OVERCOMING CONFLICT

EMBRACING THE A.R.K. METHOD TO DEFUSE ANGER, MELT RESENTMENT, AND EASE KEEN DISAPPOINTMENT

CARLA HENRY-LEWIS

DR. CAROLYN HENRY-HURST

CONTENTS

INTRODUCTION

> "All conflict can be traced back to someone's feelings getting hurt, don't you think?"

— LIANE MORIARTY

Have you ever found yourself in a situation where you and someone else just couldn't seem to see eye-to-eye? It can be frustrating when it feels like no matter how much you try to explain your viewpoint, they just don't get it, but there are ways in which we can navigate these situations without damaging our relationships with those people.

Conflict is an inevitable part of life, and it can arise in any situation—be it with a loved one or a colleague. While some conflicts can be resolved easily, others can be more challenging to deal with, especially when you don't know how to handle them. It can be overwhelming and stressful when you find yourself in such a situation, and you may feel lost and unsure of what to do. In this book, we will explore how it feels when you find yourself facing conflict with a loved one or a colleague and don't know how to deal with it. First and foremost, it is essential to acknowledge that conflict is a normal part of any relationship. However, when it arises, it can trigger a range of emotions. You may feel frustrated, angry, hurt, or even sad, and these emotions can be challenging to manage. You may replay the conflict repeatedly in your mind, wondering how it escalated and what you could have done differently. You may also feel a sense of dread or fear, wondering what the conflict means for your relationship or your work.

One of the most challenging aspects of facing conflict is not knowing how to deal with it. You may be unsure of what to say or how to express yourself, leading to a sense of helplessness and frustration. You may also fear worsening the situation, further exacerbating your anxiety. In such situations, it can be helpful to remember that conflict is an opportunity for growth and learning. While it may be uncomfortable and challenging, it can also provide an opportunity to learn more about yourself, your loved one or colleague, and your relationship. By approaching the conflict with a sense of openness and curiosity, you may be able to find a resolution that benefits everyone involved.

As a woman, you may face conflicts in various areas of your life, such as in your relationships, work, or social settings. Effective conflict resolution skills can help you to navigate these intimidating situations successfully while maintaining healthy relationships and achieving your goals. Additionally, because women are often socialized to prioritize the needs of others over their own, it may be more difficult for them to assert themselves in conflicts. Effective conflict resolution skills can help you advocate for yourself and your needs while still maintaining positive relationships with others. Women are actually an asset in the formal dispute resolution space. "Studies show that women who partake in peace processes usually focus more on reconciliation, education, transitional justice, and economic development. They also often speak up for excluded groups and the need to address underlying causes of conflict" (Fearon, 2021).

We notice that many people experience stress due to conflicts— conflicts with themselves, their children, their partner, coworkers, or even strangers. Throughout the years, we have observed this phenomenon. As children, we used to observe people as wallflowers, and we witnessed the beginning of disconnects in communication that led to misunderstandings and offenses. It seemed that people were often unaware of the disconnect that had occurred, and this is where we want to make a difference. Our goal is to teach people how to connect and provide them with the tools they need to navigate difficult situations. Although we learn the basics in school, such as our ABCs and numbers, we are not taught how to manage stress or handle conflicts effectively.

We understand how frustrating and stressful it can be when conflicts arise in our lives. It can be overwhelming and leave us feeling burned out. It's important to remember that conflict is a normal part of life, but it doesn't have to define our interactions with others. Most conflicts are simple misunderstandings that could be resolved with good communication. It takes courage to acknowledge our role in the conflict and seek resolution. By approaching conflict with empathy and a willingness to listen, we can find common ground and move forward in a positive way. If you are experiencing conflict and want to put an end to it, please know you are not alone. Seeking resolution takes strength and courage, and asking for help is okay. It's important to take care of yourself and prioritize your well-being during this process. Remember to approach the conflict with compassion for yourself and others, and focus on finding common ground. With patience, understanding, and effective communication, you can work toward a peaceful resolution and move forward with a renewed sense of positivity and growth.

It's understandable how conflicts can take a toll on various aspects of our lives. When conflicts are hampering our quality of work, mental peace, and the time we spend with our loved ones, it can be overwhelming and affect our overall well-being. You deserve to have a tension-free life at home and a clear division of work with proper direction from your management. It's important to communicate your concerns with your colleagues and management and work together to find a resolution that benefits everyone involved. Remember, you are not alone in experiencing conflicts that impact your work and personal life. It's important to prioritize self-care and seek support from loved ones or a mental health professional if needed. You deserve to have a fulfilling work-life balance and a peaceful home environment. By working toward a resolution and prioritizing your well-being, you can achieve a greater sense of peace and satisfaction in all aspects of your life.

It can be challenging to handle conflicts, and it's completely understandable if you struggle to do so. If you show emotional weakness in the face of disagreements and arguments, and your people-pleasing tendencies make you feel exasperated, please know that you are not alone. It takes time and practice to develop conflict resolution skills, and it's okay to ask for help along the way. It's important to remember that your feelings are valid, and it's okay to prioritize your well-being and needs in these situations. Remember to approach conflicts with compassion for yourself, as well as the other person involved. It's important to listen to your own needs and boundaries, while also trying to understand the other person's perspective. It's okay to take a break from the situation and come back to it with a clearer mindset. By leaning on the lessons in this book and implementing them, you can develop the tools and confidence needed to handle conflicts in a healthy and constructive way. A story is told of a man named Noah who built an ark because a flood was coming. When the rains came people climb to the highest point and still drown. Michelle Obama said "when they go low, we go high." We say you need A.R.K. to stay afloat during turbulent times.

The Key to Overcoming Conflict features the A.R.K. framework, which is designed to assist you in identifying, processing, and resolving conflicts. As this book unfolds, we will focus on the first step: identification. However, it's essential to understand that there are additional steps to process and resolve the conflict. The A.R.K. framework can help you make thoughtful and deliberate decisions in your interactions with various individuals, including family, friends, employees, and even strangers. It's important to recognize that conflict often follows a cycle, starting with a problem that may or may not be identified, with the ultimate goal being a resolution. However, when we fail to resolve the issue, it can escalate and become more complicated, eventually becoming deeply ingrained and unaddressed.

The Key to Overcoming Conflict: Embracing The A.R.K. Method To Defuse Anger, Melt Resentment, And Ease Keen Disappointment is ideal for individuals who are experiencing the adverse effects of stressful relationships on their health, who are uncertain about how they may have unintentionally offended their loved ones, resulting in reduced interaction, and those who are experiencing anger and hurt from the way they have been treated. This is your opportunity to learn how to take back control of your voice and power because, in situations of conflict, it's common to have given your power away to someone else. Discovering how to live without being offended can be incredibly beneficial in reducing stress and providing a sense of lightness and joy in life. Our assurance to you is that you will acquire the skills to identify why you become offended, as well as learn how to manage the inner conflict that arises when you do feel offended. As a result, you will experience a sense of calm and relief from stress. However, we ask that you remain receptive, prioritize your well-being, and trust the process. Sounds good?

THE A.R.K. METHOD

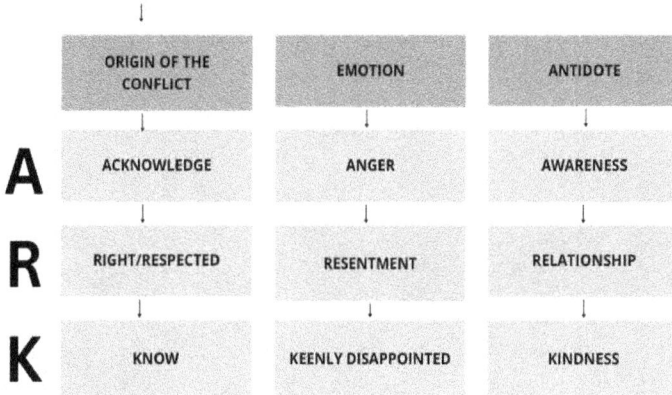

	ORIGIN OF THE CONFLICT	EMOTION	ANTIDOTE
A	ACKNOWLEDGE	ANGER	AWARENESS
R	RIGHT/RESPECTED	RESENTMENT	RELATIONSHIP
K	KNOW	KEENLY DISAPPOINTED	KINDNESS

ABOUT THE AUTHORS

We, Carolyn and Carla, are sisters who haven't always been close. We have had to resolve conflict in our relationship. It's a miracle that we are speaking to each other, much less collaborating on A.R.K. There was a time when Carla went behind Carolyn's back and made some decisions that created such a rift that we didn't speak for months. We actually had to apply the tools you will learn in this book to restore our relationship. Once you resolve conflict, relationships can be restored, and even strengthened. We have a new level of honesty and openness with each other that we didn't have before. Carolyn is an international speaker and educator. She married a pastor and has firsthand experience with conflict in the church, and the pain it causes when it is not resolved. She has two adult daughters and five grandchildren. Carla is a Relationship Doula, coach, and speaker. She is a grandmother, married, and has three adult children. She has had to resolve conflict in her marriage and even with her children. She wrote a Dear Carla column for her college newspaper. She studied psychology in college and has always been fascinated by human behavior. Her favorite pastime as a child was people-watching. That skill has been honed as she has gotten older. She sees herself as the conflict resolution guru.

PART I

ACCEPTING CONFLICT

1

UNDERSTANDING THE ROOT CAUSE OF THE CONFLICT

I wasn't always good at resolving conflict. In fact, I used to avoid it like the plague. Whenever a disagreement arose, I would do everything I could to steer clear of it. I would change the subject, pretend I didn't hear the other person, or simply walk away. But as I grew older, I realized that avoiding conflict wasn't the solution. It only made things worse. So, I decided to face my fear head-on and learn how to resolve conflicts healthily and productively. It wasn't easy, but it was worth it. You see, conflict is quite a complex and multifaceted phenomenon, and it can arise from a wide range of root causes.

Conflict stems from many places, and competition is one of the most common causes. Just as animals in the wild may fight over territory or food, we humans can also become embroiled in conflicts when we perceive our access to resources to be threatened. This can take many forms: disputes over job promotions in the workplace, money, and places of power. In some cases, that competition may be explicit and overt, such as when you and a colleague whom you have been butting heads with are vying for the same promotion. In other cases, the competition may be more subtle and implicit, such as when we feel excluded or marginalized from certain social or economic opportunities.

Second, we may be in conflict because of our sense of identity. As human beings, we are social creatures and tend to form strong attachments to our cultural, religious, ethnic, and national identities. These identities and individualities give us a sense of pride and belonging, but they can also become a source of tension and division when they clash with other people's identities. Just as different football teams may compete fiercely on the field, different groups of people may clash over their cultural or national allegiances. This can manifest in many ways, from political conflicts between different ethnic groups to religious wars between faiths to social tensions between different classes or genders.

Third, ideology. Just as different religions or cultures may have competing values and beliefs, different political or philosophical ideologies can clash. This can lead to conflicts over issues such as human rights, economic systems, environmental policies, and geopolitical strategies. For example, some people may believe that capitalism is the best way to create prosperity and freedom, while others may argue that socialism or communism is a more equitable and sustainable alternative. These differing ideologies may lead to heated debates, protests, and even violence.

A fourth root cause of conflict is power. Just as animals in a pack may jostle for dominance, humans can also become embroiled in disputes over power and hierarchy. This can take many forms, from struggles between individuals or groups for control of institutions or resources, to conflicts between nations over geopolitical influence. In some cases, the struggle for power may be overt and violent, such as in a coup or a war. In other cases, it may be more subtle and symbolic, such as when people compete for social status or recognition.

Understanding the root causes of conflict in our relationships is like shining a light on the dark corners of our minds. It allows us to see the hidden fears, insecurities, and unmet needs that often drive our behavior. By acknowledging and addressing these underlying issues, we can break free from the cycle of blame and defensiveness that so often characterizes conflict. Instead, we can approach our relationships with greater empathy, compassion, and understanding, creating a safe space for open and honest communication. This newfound awareness can also help us to recognize patterns of behavior that may be contributing to the conflict, allowing us to make positive changes and cultivate healthier dynamics.

PHASES OF CONFLICT

Imagine this: There's a pot of water on the stove. At first glance, the water seems calm and still. But as the heat is turned up, tiny bubbles start to form and rise to the surface. These bubbles may seem harmless at first, but if left unattended, they can quickly turn into a rolling boil. It works just the same with conflict and unproductive behaviors in our relationships; they don't just appear out of nowhere. They start off as small and meaningless, gradually building up like those bubbles in a pot of water over time. And just like boiling water, these conflicts can cause a lot of damage if we do not address them early on. That's why it's important to understand the different stages of relationship drama. These stages may not be linear, but they are identifiable. By recognizing them, we can be on our way to building healthier and more sustainable relationships at work and in our personal lives.

Stage 1: Prelude Stage

In relationships and at work, some things will happen that allow the conflict to arise, but I want to mention that just because these certain conditions exist, it does not necessarily mean that the conflict will arise. Let's take a look at why communication is the biggest contributor to conflict.

I have gained a lot of insight and wisdom over the years through the work that I do, and the one thing I have found after all these years is that most conflict starts bubbling because of misunderstandings, or things that should have been said but were left unsaid. Here's an example: Margret, your new manager, has just onboarded a new client for a big project, and in all her excitement, she has asked you to be on her team because she knows you're brilliant and will help lead the team to success. The only problem is that she has been incredibly vague about the goals and KPIs of the whole project, so you go ahead and tackle the project in the best way you know how, and halfway through the project, she checks in on your work, only to tell you that you completely missed the plot. If we're being honest, this is the kind of behavior that would make anyone lose composure, especially if you've already invested extra time outside of your normal working hours to work on the project.

Or let's use another example: Imagine your partner comes home one evening and asks you to bake a cake for their boss. The staff is planning a surprise office party for him, and they thought it would be thoughtful to bake something, rather than order a store-bought cake. You're an excellent baker, and he offered to ask you to help, and you're thrilled at the idea.

At first glance, this may seem like a straightforward request, but many potential miscommunications could lead to conflict. For example, you may assume that your partner wants you to bake the cake that evening, but the party is not until the end of the week. Alternatively, you may assume that your partner wants you to bake a simple chocolate cake, but in reality, they were hoping for a more complex and decorated cake. These kinds of misunderstandings can easily lead to frustration and conflict. Also, we need to consider that communication goes far beyond just the words we say. The tone of our voice, our body language, and even the context in which we say things can all influence how the message is received. In this case of the cake, your partner may be rushed and ask you hurriedly to bake it, causing tension and stress. Alternatively, they may ask you calmly and casually, making the request seem more like a suggestion. These subtle differences in communication can significantly impact how we feel about the request and whether we are willing to help.

Experience has also taught me that cultural and linguistic differences can also complicate communication. If you and your partner come from different backgrounds, you may have different communication styles and expectations. For example, some cultures value direct and straightforward communication, while others value more indirect and subtle communication. These differences can lead to misunderstandings and conflicts, particularly if one partner assumes that the other is being rude or disrespectful when they are simply communicating in a different way.

Something of note is about 15-20% of the population is neuro-divergent and they communicate differently. Hence, much of the advice shared about conflict resolution does not work well with this population.

Stage 2: Triggering Events

Have you ever played Jenga? You know, the game where you stack blocks on top of each other, taking turns pulling one block out at a time until the tower comes crashing down? Well, relationships at work and in life are a lot like that game. Each block represents a different event or circumstance that can trigger conflict.

Sometimes, it might be a small block, like a miscommunication or an unmet expectation. Other times, it might be a bigger block, like a disagreement about values or a major life event. And just like in Jenga, the more blocks you add, the more unstable the tower becomes.

But here's the thing: unlike Jenga, relationships aren't just a game. They're an essential part of our lives, and conflicts can have real consequences. That's why it's so important to understand what triggers conflict and how to navigate it when it arises.

So, if you're ready to become a Jenga master of relationships, let's explore some of the most common triggers of conflict in relationships and the workplace, and how we can handle them with wit and a whole lot of grace.

In Romantic Relationships

If you've ever been in a relationship, then you know that every couple experiences a bit of conflict, and that is not necessarily a bad thing. Anytime two independent adults kind of merge into one unit, there is going to be a clash somewhere, differences in opinion are going to arise, and there are also going to be times when one person feels they are not being listened to by their partner. Let's have a look at some of the causes of conflict in relationships.

Selfishness

Sometimes, we tend to get so wrapped up in our own little worlds and desires that we forget how our actions truly affect the lives of those we love the most. Sure, it's important to honor our wiring and listen to our own needs, but we also have to find that place of balance where we are able to see and respect the needs of our partners.

Resentment

Resentment in a relationship can be compared to a small spark in a dry forest. At first, it seems insignificant and manageable, but as time passes and the resentment grows, it can quickly ignite into a raging wildfire of conflict. Just as a wildfire devastates everything in its path, resentment can destroy the foundation of trust and love that we built in our relationship. We need to remember that just as it takes a lot of effort and resources to put out a wildfire, it takes a lot of work and communication to address and resolve the underlying issues that fuel resentment in a relationship. If left unaddressed, resentment can ultimately lead to the demise of a relationship, much like a wildfire can leave behind a barren and desolate landscape.

We all have to understand that if we don't take it upon ourselves to set small boundaries along the way in our relationships, we're going to be building an ever-growing pile of resentment that is going to grow so big it eventually ruins the entire thing. No relationship is going to feel 100 percent good all the time; our partners are eventually going to do something that triggers us because they're humans. Humans are flawed in that sense, so it's important that we go ahead and set the necessary boundaries around their behavior. If we don't, we internalize the pain without giving ourselves a full opportunity to process it, and we create unhealthy conditions for engagement in our relationships.

Here are a few tips on what we can do to work through the resentment in our relationships:

- **Meet yourself from a place of compassion.** What you're feeling is not inherently bad, and it does not make you a bad person. Resentment is a messenger, and it's trying to tell us that something is very important to us. Be kind to yourself as you work on understanding and figuring out what's missing.
- **Identify what's missing.** Become fiercely curious about your needs. What do you perceive as having been completely unfair to you throughout the whole situation?
- **Look for ways through which you can fulfill that need or desire.** People won't always know what we need or what we want, so we have to be forthright about telling them that. Or alternatively, you can take care of that need for yourself. What adjustments do you need to make in your life to improve the situation? What kinds of boundaries can you enforce?
- **Have realistic expectations in place.** Is your partner not meeting your expectations because they're overly unrealistic? If we have unrealistic expectations, we're somehow always going to end up feeling like there's something missing, so the disappointment won't end.
- **Let go of what you need to let go.** Holding on to anger or bitterness is not at all helpful. The more we focus on those situations, the more we will go out to look for evidence to support and strengthen those claims and

allegations. Rather, choose to work through those issues and nudge yourself to move on.

Power Dynamics and Control

Sometimes, in relationships, our partners want to have complete control over us and what we do—this is typically a dynamic that happens when one person enjoys feeling superior. Here are some examples:

• **Financial control:**

If one partner in the relationship controls all the finances, it can lead to an imbalance of power that causes dissatisfaction. For example, if one earns significantly more money than the other and controls all the finances, the one who earns less may feel like they are not being treated as an equal partner in the relationship. Also, if one partner uses money as a tool to control or manipulate the other partner, it creates a very toxic power dynamic that is damaging to the relationship. This behavior is dangerous and a red flag. This could be a circumstance when you give up on resolving conflict and simply leave the relationship.

• **Decision-making control:**

If you and your partner don't communicate about important decisions in the relationship and consult each other, it can create a power imbalance that is a breeding ground for resentment. Let's say your partner never really lets you decide where you eat for date night, what activities you'll do on the weekends, and how you spend your free time together, you—the one who is being pushed to the backseat—are going to start feeling like you are not a valued person in the relationship. The feelings of frustration are going to bubble up, and at some point, they're going to explode in a fit of rage!

Here are some ways in which you and your partner can work toward having a more balanced and equal power dynamic:

- **Keep arguments and communication respectful.**

If you want your partner to understand your needs, then it is only fair for you to work on understanding their needs as well. If you are in a situation where you feel that your partner is overlooking your needs, you can try saying something like:

"I feel like you could be more supportive about…"

"It's starting to come across as if I am disappointing you on X, Y, and Z. Can we clarify and discuss what our mutual expectations of each other are?" Making that mutual commitment to one another to listen to each other will help the both of you avoid hurting each other.

- **Be open about your vulnerabilities to one another.**

If your partner cares about you as much as they say they do, then they will work hard at ensuring that you feel seen and heard in the relationship. For example, if you feel really vulnerable about your body, then be honest and open with your partner about that. Trust that they will love you enough to not use that against you. Here's a potential example of what you can say to them: "I feel really self-conscious now that I have gained weight. I am worried that you are checking other people out, and then comparing them to me." A kind and gentle response to this would be something like: "I am so sorry that you feel that way, I am going to work a little harder at reminding you how remarkably breathtaking I find you," and not something along the lines of, "Oh, but if you're so self-conscious about how you look, why not go to the gym or something."

- **Be willing to compromise.**

Relationships are about equal give and take. You can't always get your way, and they won't always get their way. When it comes to compromise, it's important to keep in mind both your and your partner's strengths and preferences. Here are some examples of what compromise in a relationship might look like:

○ This or that kind of situation: This can look like I'll do this for you, and you do that for me. Both of you do something for the other person that you wouldn't typically do. For example, I'll cook dinner if you do the dishes.

○ Taking turns to do things: Do it your way this time and then do it their way the next time. For example, you choose the restaurant this time, and they choose the restaurant next time. You do holidays with one family this time and then a holiday with their family the next time.

Meeting each other in the middle: You both sacrifice just a little bit to honor both of your desires and needs. For example, if they prefer warmer temperatures and you prefer cooler temperatures, you could have the thermostat set somewhere in between so that neither of you is uncomfortable.

In the Workplace

Ah, the joys of working with others. Collaborating on projects, sharing ideas, and building relationships can be incredibly rewarding. But let's face it, workplace conflicts are bound to happen. Whether it's a disagreement over priorities, a clash of personalities, or a miscommunication, tensions can quickly escalate and disrupt productivity. So, what are the triggers that ignite these conflicts? Buckle up, because we're about to explore the common culprits that turn coworkers into combatants.

Personality Differences

Personality clashes in the workplace can be as entertaining as they are frustrating. It's like watching an episode of *Survivor* but with less tropical scenery and more office politics. There's that overly chatty colleague who can't seem to stop talking about her weekend, the micromanager who insists on approving every email you send out, and the know-it-all who's always quick to correct and scrutinize your grammar. Oh, and dear me, let us not forget about the introvert who just wants to be left alone in peace with their spreadsheets, or the extrovert who wants to turn every meeting into a social event. It truly is a miracle that we get anything done at all. It's like trying to fit a square peg into a round hole. Or, even better, like trying to convince a cat to take a bath. It's a battle that nobody wins. So, what's the solution?

Well, we can start off by understanding ourselves and our own unique personality traits and quirks because we are then able to accept ourselves from a place without judgment. Only then are we able to try to understand everybody else's uniqueness and idiosyncrasies.

Or, you stock up on noise-canceling headphones and hope for the best. Just kidding; what you can do is learn to embrace what other people bring to the table. What are some of the things that your colleagues are good at? Or even better, think about how you can use those personality traits to find the good. For example, if one of your coworkers has a very aggressive style of communication, consider that as something that allows for direct communication, so the next time you need honest feedback about a project that you've been working on, you can approach and ask them for honest input and feedback. Or, if you have one of those colleagues who never seems to give any pushback in discussions, think about it as their way of choosing to show empathy; they're trying their best to understand where everyone else is coming from with their suggestions and feedback.

Don't tiptoe around conflict. One of the hardest things that comes with learning to gel well with different personalities in the workplace is handling conflict maturely. So, the next time you get into a dispute with one of your colleagues, don't be afraid to confront them rather than going behind their back and discussing it with a colleague.

Focus on the shared goals, rather than your own personal agendas. You and your colleagues are all on the same team, and you're all working on the same goals. This is the whole idea behind the phenomenon of being a team player. Being on a team does not mean that you have to sacrifice your own opinion—it ultimately just means you have to prioritize the ultimate purpose of being on that team.

Unrealistic Expectations

Ah, the sweet aroma of unrealistic expectations in the workplace. It's like the smell of freshly brewed coffee but with a hint of burnt toast as a side. We've all been there. You're given a task with an impossible deadline or asked to produce a project with limited resources. And when you don't meet these expectations, all hell breaks loose. Suddenly, your boss is breathing down your neck like a hungry dragon, and your coworkers are throwing shade like it's a beach volleyball tournament. It's enough to make you want to throw your laptop out the window and run away to join the circus. But let's face it, the circus probably has its own set of unrealistic expectations as well. What could the solution to all of this possibly be?

Well, firstly, you can simply just invest in a stress ball and hope for the best—just kidding. I think, in some way or another, we're all simply just trying to survive that toxic game of unrealistic expectations being imposed on us, one slice of burnt toast at a time. I believe the first thing that we can do to manage expectations is to communicate our limitations effectively.

Now, before you think to yourself, *This is going to get me fired,* you can relax because I am going to show you exactly how you can do it diplomatically and assertively.

- **Be unapologetically confident.**

Here's the thing—you're never going to come across as that fearless and empowered employee if you're constantly drenching everything you say in a thick layer of sugar syrup. Sometimes it just helps to state things as they are. It will become far easier for you to stand up for yourself when you understand the value that you bring to the table. Affirm that belief in yourself by using "I" statements when you're making a point. Use those "I" statements like "I deserve to be listened to" because, in actuality, you really do deserve to be listened to.

- **Ask for what you want.**

You don't always have to be a "Yes, ma'am" employee. And you have to remember that if you don't ask for what you want, you're never going to get it. Be simple and concise about your ideas and your opinions. You also don't have to add a layer of apology every time you make a request.

- **Be adamant about your emotional boundaries.**

By emotional boundaries, I mean telling yourself that you are not going to allow your day to be messed up by someone in a foul mood. We all have those colleagues who wake up on the wrong side of the bed, and just because things aren't going well for them, they expect things to be the same for everyone else around them. So, let your colleagues and bosses know how you would like to send and receive feedback. Delegate tasks where necessary (you do not have to be the office superhero) and focus on creating a schedule that prioritizes work-life balance.

- **Enforce your mental boundaries.**

Your mental energy at work matters, and if you want to continue doing the best work that you can do, you need to know exactly when and how you're going to set it. Here's what you can do:

 You set your working hours, and you stick to them.

 Encourage management to run meetings more efficiently. In other words, if you feel that they are unnecessarily making you and your colleagues spend time in meetings, let them know.

 Do not entertain all that small office gossip going around. You can so easily land yourself in trouble with that.

Competition

The workplace can be a jungle! At a superficial glance, it can seem like everyone is at peace and in harmony with one another, but one wrong move and a predator might just pounce at you. Healthy competition is good because it's incredibly motivating, but too much of it can cause a team to come apart at the seams. You want that same promotion that Cindy is up for, and pretty soon, both of you start sabotaging each other's work and efforts—hardly the recipe for growth, is it? Here are some tips to think over to help manage that workplace competition:

- **Focus on collaboration, not competition.** Encourage each other to work together toward a common goal rather than competing against each other. Build an environment where collaboration is valued and rewarded, and where everyone feels like they are working toward a shared purpose.
- **Celebrate each other's successes.** Sure, it's going to be hard to put up a smile when Janet gets that promotion that you've been gunning for, but you can still be happy for them—it won't kill you.
- **Encourage open communication.** Communication is key to managing competition in the workplace. Be open and honest with each other about all your goals, strengths, and weaknesses. This will help to create a more supportive and collaborative work environment.
- **Set clear expectations.** If you are leading a project, make sure that everyone on the team understands what is expected of them. This will help to reduce the likelihood of misunderstandings and conflicts arising from differences in expectations.
- **Lead by example.** You gotta demonstrate the kind of behavior you want to see from your coworkers and model the kind of collaboration and teamwork that you hope to foster in the workplace.

Poor Communication

The problem of miscommunication in the workplace can often lead to conflicts between colleagues. While some disputes may arise from minor issues like a colleague microwaving their fish lunch in the cafeteria, some arise from much bigger issues, like not briefing a colleague about an important deadline or leaving them in the dark when you're supposed to be collaborating on a project. With that said, let's take a look at the various stages that we're likely to encounter when in conflict with someone.

INITIATION PHASE

The initiation phase of the conflict can be likened to soup slowly simmering on the stove. At first, all is calm and well (sort of), but as the heat slowly gets turned up, the soup begins to bubble and boil, and just like soup can easily bubble over, conversations can turn pretty ugly quite quickly, spiral out of control, and leave an aftermath of hurt feelings and broken relationships. Here are five things that are more than likely to happen in that initiation phase of conflict:

1. **The "I'm Right, You're Wrong" Dance:** This is where you and the other person would likely be doing a bit of back and forth on whose fault and whose actions started the whole conundrum. It's like a bad version of the tango, where instead of dancing, both of you are just trying to prove a point. It's a dance that nobody wins, and quite frankly, both of you just look silly.

2. **The "Who Started It?" Blame Game:** When the chips fall, everyone wants to know who started it. It's like kindergarten, but instead of fighting over toys, you're fighting over who insulted whom first. Spoiler alert: nobody wins this game, either.

3. **The "Let's Get Our Allies Involved" Party:** When things get really heated, both of you start calling up your buddies and work besties because someone has to have your back. It's like a game of telephone, but instead of passing on a message, you're passing on your anger; it's that office party that nobody wants to attend, but everybody gets dragged into it because of "work policy."

4. **The "Let's Make a List of Grievances" Brainstorm:** This is where you both start making a list of all the things that you're angry about. You can actually go so far as to compare it to a brainstorming session, but instead of coming up with ideas, you're both just coming up with reasons for more things to be mad about. Another spoiler alert: nobody really wants to read those lists, either!

5. **The "Let's See Who Blinks First" Staring Contest:** It's like two kiddos on a playground, staring each other down, waiting to see who blinks first. It's a contest that nobody wins, but in which everybody ends up with a headache.

The thing about initiating conflict is that when it's poorly executed, the consequences can be disastrous. We need to be able to rationally approach the situation so that the overall outcome can be productive. Here are five things to keep in mind during this initiation phase of conflict:

1. **Try not to let your emotions take over:** It's important to keep your cool during the initiation phase of the conflict. Don't let your emotions get the best of you, or you might end up saying or doing something you regret. Remember, there is no rewind or take-back button when it comes to the things that come out of our mouths. Once it's out there, it's out. So, take a deep breath, count to ten, and remember that cooler heads always prevail.

2. **Listen to the other side's perspective:** It's easy to get caught up in your own point of view during a conflict because you feel like you have been wronged and the person needs to see this, but it's important to listen to the other side's perspective as well. You might learn something new or realize there's more to the situation than you originally thought.

3. **Don't make assumptions:** When conflict arises, it's easy to jump to conclusions and make assumptions about the other person's intentions or motivations. However, assumptions can be dangerous and often lead to misunderstandings. Instead, ask questions and seek clarification to avoid making false assumptions.

4. **Let respect lead the conversation:** Communication is key during a conflict, but it's important to communicate in a clear and respectful manner. Avoid using aggressive or defensive language, and try to use "I" statements

instead of "you" statements to express your feelings and concerns.

5. **Focus on finding solutions, not just winning the argument:** In the heat of the moment, it's easy to get caught up in trying to prove your point and "win" the argument. However, it's important to remember that conflict resolution should be about finding a solution that works for everyone involved, not just about winning the argument. Keep an open mind, be willing to compromise, and work together to find a solution that everyone can agree on.

DIFFERENTIATION PHASE

So, you know when you're arguing with someone, and you both have your own opinions, but you're not quite sure what the other person's opinion is? That's where the differentiation phase comes in. It's the part of the argument where you start to understand the other person's point of view and vice versa. Think of it as the "I see where you're coming from" phase.

But let's be real, this phase isn't always easy to navigate. It's like trying to untangle a bunch of cords without getting them mixed up. You have to listen, ask questions, and really try to understand where the other person is coming from. It's not just about winning the argument; it's about gaining a deeper understanding of the issue at hand.

And let's not forget about the emotions that come into play during this phase. It's like a rollercoaster ride. One minute you're feeling frustrated, and the next minute you're feeling empathetic. It's like a game of emotional Jenga where you have to carefully remove certain blocks without causing the tower to collapse.

Let's take a look at common behaviors that you may see play out in the differentiation phase of the conflict.

- **The ego on steroids behavior:** This is where everyone suddenly thinks they're the best thing to happen since sliced bread and their ideas should be treated like gold. Here's an example: "I don't care what anyone else thinks, my idea is the best!"
- **More opinions than a talk radio show:** All of a sudden, everyone has an opinion, and they all want to be heard at the same time. Here's an example: "I think we should do it my way!" "No, my way is better!" "But what about my opinion?!"
- **Cheese grater words:** The conflict gets sharper, and everyone involved starts using their words like a cheese grater on a block of cheddar. *Ouch.* Here's an example: "What were you thinking? Are you an idiot?" "Who died and made you the boss?"
- **Polar bear parties:** As everyone starts to differentiate, it's not uncommon to see groups of people breaking off into their own little cliques, like polar bears huddling up for warmth. Here's an example: "I'm not sitting with them; I don't agree with their approach."
- **The blame game:** What would conflict be without a little game of tennis blame? When people feel strongly about their ideas, it's easy for them to start pointing

fingers at everyone else. Here's an example: "If we fail, it's all because you didn't listen to me!"

Tips on Overcoming the Differentiation Phase

- **Practice active listening:**

The first step to successfully navigating the differentiation phase of the conflict is to actively listen to the other person. This means giving them your full attention, asking clarifying questions, and seeking to understand their perspective. By listening actively, you can show the other person that you value their thoughts and feelings, which can help to build trust and create a more collaborative atmosphere.

- **Focus on the issue, not the person:**

When conflicts arise, it's easy to get caught up in personal attacks and blame. However, to make it through the differentiation phase successfully, it's important to focus on the issue at hand, rather than attacking the other person. Keep the conversation centered on the problem you are trying to solve, and avoid making personal attacks or assumptions about the other person.

- **Communicate clearly and respectfully:**

Effective communication is key to successfully navigating the differentiation phase of the conflict. Be clear and direct in your communication, but also be respectful and considerate of the other person's feelings. Avoid using aggressive or confrontational language, and instead, focus on using "I" statements to express your own thoughts and feelings.

- **Stay open to new ideas:**

One of the biggest challenges in the differentiation phase of the conflict is staying open to new ideas and perspectives. It's easy to become entrenched in your own point of view, but this can make it difficult to find a resolution. Instead, try to stay open-minded and flexible, and be willing to consider new ideas and approaches.

- **Seek outside help if necessary:**

Sometimes, despite your best efforts, conflicts can escalate and become difficult to resolve. In these cases, it can be helpful to seek outside help from a mediator, counselor, or another neutral third party. These professionals can provide an objective perspective and help you find a resolution that works for everyone involved.

RESOLUTION STAGE

I like to think of this stage as the one where everyone hugs and starts singing "Kumbaya" together. It's that pot of soup that's been simmering on the stove for hours, with all the flavors melding together to create something delicious. It's like a symphony that reaches its crescendo, with all the instruments playing in perfect harmony. It's like a game of Jenga, where the tower is teetering on the brink of collapse, but somehow, miraculously, it all stays standing.

It's the happy ending we all crave, the moment of catharsis that makes everything that came before worth it. Okay, I'm going to stop right here because maybe I might have over-exaggerated a bit, because the resolution stage does not always end with everyone hugging it out, singing some "Kumbaya," and basking in the warm glow of resolution. And this is why:

- **The "Sorry, Not Sorry" Approach:**

Look, some people are really stubborn, so rather than stepping up and wearing their big-person pants, the one common mistake that we sometimes make in conflict resolution is offering a half-hearted apology. You know the type: "I'm sorry if I hurt your feelings, but you were being really annoying." This approach is like trying to put out a fire with gasoline. It might seem like you're making an effort to resolve the conflict, but you're really just making things worse by deflecting blame and minimizing the other person's feelings. Remember, the moment you add a "but" to an apology, it loses all substance and meaning.

- **The "Passive-Aggressive" Maneuver:**

Why not just jab at the person? Another common mistake I see people make when they are attempting to make amends is that they throw some passive-aggressive behaviors right into the mix. This can be in the form of making sarcastic comments, giving the silent treatment, or making subtle yet snarky comments about the other person's character. Sure, it may feel satisfying in the moment, and make you feel all mighty and powerful, but it's not going to help you reach a resolution. In fact, the chance that the conflict could escalate even further is highly likely.

- **The "Win-At-All-Costs" Attitude:**

Conflict resolution is not some game or race to be won; it's simply about coming to a consensus so that there is harmony again, but some people don't approach it that way. They want to "win" the argument at all costs, even if it means hurting the other person or compromising their own values. This approach is like playing a game of chess with a bulldozer. You may feel like you're making progress, but you're really just bulldozing over the other person's feelings and needs.

- **The "Blame Game" Strategy:**

We've mentioned earlier that when conflicts arise, it's easy to fall into the trap of blaming the other person for everything that's gone wrong. This approach is like trying to solve a Rubik's Cube by smashing it with a hammer. Sure, you may feel like you're making progress, but you're really just destroying the puzzle and making it impossible to solve.

- **The "Avoidance" Tactic:**

There's a lot that I have learned about avoidance over the years, and some of the main reasons why we choose to go that route are

> We may have grown up in environments where talking about our feelings wasn't acceptable, so we tend to hold back on what we're truly feeling or what we want to say.
> We're naturally used to being avoidant when it comes to our feelings and emotions. Our needs were neglected in childhood, so, therefore, we've just taught ourselves to stay as agreeable as possible.
> Sometimes, we really just aren't all that mad anymore. We're choosing to pick our battles wisely and would rather not expend valuable and precious energy on small things; our peace of mind matters most and is so much more valuable.

Either way, conflict sucks, and it feels downright uncomfortable, so it's understandable why some of us may pretend that we're fine, sweep our feelings under the rug, or simply refuse to engage in any meaningful dialogue. This approach is like trying to plant a garden in a desert. Sure, you may be able to grow something for a little while, but eventually, the lack of water and nutrients will make the plants wither and die. Acknowledging your frustration or your anger, or whatever emotion it is that you're feeling, is a powerful tool in ensuring that we set the necessary boundaries with the people we need to set boundaries with. Some helpful statements that can help you take a more proactive, rather than an avoidant, approach when dealing with conflict resolution are as follows:

- Your "I am not mad" can be turned into "I was really hurt by the things you said and the way you acted."
- "Leave me alone" can turn into "Please just give me some space and some time to cool down so that I can think about what happened."
- "It's all good" can become "I want to let this go, but I just cannot bring myself to do that."
- "There is nothing to talk about" can be turned into "I don't think I have the energy to deal with that right now. Please just give me a moment."

More Tips on How to Successfully Navigate the Resolution Stage

- **Take a deep breath and count to 10.** Or 20. Or a 100. Whatever it takes to keep yourself from going full Hulk mode. Remember, the resolution requires a level head, not a smashed coffee mug.
- **Listen, listen, listen.** That means no interrupting, no eye-rolling, and definitely no checking your phone. Give the other person your full attention, even if you'd rather be watching paint dry.
- **Use "I" statements instead of "you" statements.** Saying, "You always do this!" is a surefire way to put the other person on the defensive. Instead, try "I feel frustrated when this happens." It's simple, it's effective,

and it won't make you sound like a finger-pointing toddler.

- **Find common ground.** It's hard to stay mad at someone when you bond over your love of cheesy '90s sitcoms. Or dogs. Or a mutual hatred of cilantro. Whatever it is, look for something you can both agree on and use it as a jumping-off point for finding a solution.

- **Don't be afraid to apologize.** Even if you don't feel like you're the one in the wrong, a well-timed "I'm sorry" can go a long way toward defusing a tense situation. Just make sure you're apologizing for your part in the conflict, not for the fact that it happened in the first place. And if all else fails, offer to buy the other person a drink. It's not a solution, but it's a start!

BIASES IN CONFLICT RESOLUTION

Imagine: Two people are in the middle of a heated argument, and both of them are convinced that they're right and the other person is wrong. Now, imagine that a mediator steps in to resolve the conflict, but they have a secret bias: They're convinced that the best way to settle any disagreement is through a game of rock-paper-scissors. Suddenly, the argument turns strange as the mediator suggests they settle the dispute with a friendly game. But wait, what if one person has a rock-paper-scissors bias, and the other is more of a coin-flipper? Oh, the biases we bring to conflict resolution can be so silly and unpredictable!

The thing with biases is that they are a lot like a pair of tinted glasses we wear when we view the world around us. They can distort our perception and make us see things in a certain way, whether that way is accurate or not. When it comes to conflict resolution, biases can play a major role in how we interpret the situation, how we communicate with the other party, and what solutions we propose.

Let's take, for example, two people from different cultures who have a conflict over a perceived slight. If one person is biased against the other's culture, they may see the situation as a deliberate act of disrespect rather than an honest misunderstanding. This can cause them to react defensively and escalate the conflict further, rather than taking the time to understand the other person's perspective and find a mutually beneficial solution.

Also, biases affect how we listen to and interpret the other person's words and actions. If we have a bias against someone, we may be more likely to assume the worst about their intentions and overlook any positive gestures they make. This can make it difficult to build trust and find common ground.

The reality is that biases can make conflict resolution more difficult because they cloud our judgment, hinder our ability to see the situation objectively, and make it harder for us to communicate effectively. To resolve conflicts successfully, we need to be aware of the biases that put a veil over our judgment and work to overcome them.

Let's take a look at the different types of biases that can sometimes get in our way.

- **Confirmation bias:**

This is when someone only seeks out information that confirms their pre-existing beliefs rather than considering alternative viewpoints. For example, if you're convinced that your coworker is lazy, you might only pay attention to the times when they're not working rather than acknowledging the times when they are.

- **Anchoring bias:**

This is when someone relies too heavily on the first piece of information they receive, and it influences their decision-making going forward. For example, if you're negotiating a salary with a potential employer and they offer you a lowball number, you might be anchored to that number and have a hard time negotiating a higher one.

- **Halo effect bias:**

This is when someone makes an overall judgment about someone based on a single trait or characteristic. For example, if you meet someone who's really funny, you might assume that they're also smart, kind, and talented, even if you haven't seen any evidence of those traits.

- **Fundamental attribution error:**

This is when we attribute someone else's behavior to their personality or character, rather than considering external factors that may have influenced their behavior. For instance, when someone cuts you off in traffic, you might assume they're a bad driver or a rude person, rather than considering the possibility they're in a hurry or didn't see you.

I also remember this one morning, I wanted to catch up on some emails and headed out to the nearby bakery. About 10 minutes after I had arrived, a group of what seemed to be tourists walked in and saw the man sitting opposite my table spill his juice all over. As you would think, one of them immediately assumed that the man was a clumsy and careless wreck, but there was a sweet young lady who made a comment about him having a rough morning and offered to help clean up. Later on, they came to find out that the man had just received some devastating news and was struggling to keep it together. The first friend realized the error of their judgment, and at that moment, you could see their face changing because they came to understand the importance of empathy and understanding. I assume the sweet young lady who helped must've been rather proud of herself and her ability to see beyond a simple mistake (bless her parents for raising such an angel).

It just goes to show that we never truly know what someone else is going through, and it's always better to give them the benefit of the doubt. A person is more than one simple mistake that they make in a moment of poor judgment.

- **Sunk cost fallacy:**

This is when we continue to invest time, money, or energy into something that is clearly not working out; it's mainly because we've already poured so much into this particular thing that letting it all go would make us seem a little bit idiotic. I mean, if you've spent weeks working on a presentation and it's not working out like you want it to, you might keep trying to salvage it or ignoring any other advice that your colleagues offer because you don't want to feel like you've wasted your time and effort.

Of course, while these biases can be amusing to think about, they can also be serious obstacles to effective conflict resolution. It's important to be aware of these biases and try to overcome them to find a fair and constructive solution. Here are some handy solutions to help you overcome with the best of them.

- **Recognize when you might be a little biased.**

Back in the days during my intern years, bless me, I was trying to solve a problem at work and noticed that my initial reaction was to side with my friend—who was clearly in the wrong, mind you. After reflecting on the whole situation, I realized that I was biased toward my friend because of the close relationship we had outside of work. It's really important that you acknowledge that you have biases because sometimes they influence our judgment when we're attempting to resolve conflicts. Remember, too, that biases are not a reflection of your character, or you as a person, but simply a product of your experiences and beliefs.

- **Perspectives are important.**

I mean, if you're always arguing with a coworker or a partner about a consensus when collaborating, the problem is most likely you're not willing to listen to one another. A crucial part of resolving conflicts is understanding where everyone is coming from. When you listen to each person's perspective, you can see the situation from various angles and make a more informed decision.

- **Separate the facts from the opinions.**

While opinions are important, it's essential to separate them from the facts when you're trying to resolve a conflict. Doing so will help you focus on finding a solution based on what's actually happening rather than personal beliefs or assumptions.

- **Stay open-minded.**

You must be willing to consider new information and perspectives, even if they challenge your beliefs. If someone comes up with an alternative solution, instead of downright dismissing their idea, ask them to explain their reasoning. You will learn a lot and perhaps be able to devise a compromise that satisfies both of you.

- **Solutions, solutions, solutions.**

Ultimately, the goal of conflict resolution is to find a solution that works for everyone involved. While it's important to acknowledge where mistakes were made, placing blame is as helpful as a broken matchstick. Instead, focus on finding ways to move forward and prevent similar conflicts from occurring in the future. There was a time when I had a disagreement with a family member who had borrowed my laptop without asking. Instead of getting angry and accusatory, I explained why I was upset and suggested that we develop a system for sharing electronic belongings in the future. We were able to move past the issue and resolve it, which helped prevent similar occurrences from happening down the line.

2

BALANCE BEFORE IT ESCALATES

One time, I got into a disagreement with a friend over something silly. I can't even remember what it was about, but I do remember that we both got pretty hot and bothered about it. The whole thing started off as just a minor disagreement. But then, things started to escalate. I raised my voice, and my friend raised hers. We started interrupting each other, and pretty soon, we were both talking over each other at the same time.

Before long, we were both so caught up in the argument that we weren't even making sense anymore. We were just yelling and getting angrier by the second. Finally, I realized how absurd the whole thing was. I mean, we were arguing about something so trivial, and yet we were both acting like it was a life-or-death situation. So, I took a deep breath and said, "You know what? This is getting out of hand. Let's just agree to disagree and move on." My friend hesitated for a moment, still looking angry. But then she took a deep breath too, and said, "Yeah, you're right. This isn't worth getting so worked up over, and I wouldn't want to lose a lifelong bestie because of something trivial."

I felt a wave of relief wash over me. It honestly felt like having a glass of water after a long run, so we both calmed down and moved on from the argument. And looking back on the whole situation now, I can't help but laugh at how silly we both must have looked, getting so worked up over something so trivial.

What did I learn after this whole ordeal? When it comes to conflicts, it's important to keep things in perspective. It's normal to get angry or frustrated sometimes, but it's not worth escalating the situation and making things worse. Sometimes, the best thing to do is just take a step back, breathe, and let it go.

THE PHASES OF CONFLICT ESCALATION

It all started with a harmless comment. Maybe your friend mentioned that they don't like pineapple on pizza. You, being a die-hard pineapple enthusiast, took offense and fired back with a witty comeback. But your friend was not feeling your humor and fired back with an insult.

Both of you were on edge, and that's where the conflict had officially begun. It was like a game of verbal table tennis, with each of you trying to one-up the other. But then, things started to get personal. Your friend mentioned that you spilled salsa on your shirt at a party, and suddenly it was not about pizza anymore, but about your dignity.

At that point, both of you were fully committed to the argument. Your friend started exaggerating their points, and you did the same. A battle of hyperbole had begun, with each of you attempting to outdo the other. "You always do this!" "No, *you* always do this!"

And then, just when you thought things couldn't get any worse, someone brings up politics. Suddenly, you're not just arguing about pizza and spilled salsa, you're arguing about the fate of the world. It's like a game of telephone, with each of you repeating the same talking points you heard on cable news.

Eventually, the conflict reached its boiling point. You're both shouting at the top of your lungs, and nothing is getting resolved. It was like a scene from a bad sitcom, with each of you trying to deliver the final punchline. But then, something strange happened. You both start laughing hysterically, tears rolling down your face like sweat after a long run. Maybe it's because the situation was so ridiculous, or maybe it's because you both realized how silly the argument was in the first place.

Either way, the conflict de-escalated, and you were both left feeling slightly embarrassed. But at least you learned something important: Never underestimate the power of pizza to bring people together.

It's so easy for conflict to escalate. And most of the time, it happens without us realizing how bad things are actually getting. Each phase of conflict escalation, the same as with the conflict resolution stage, has unique challenges and characteristics of its own.

- **Phase 1: The "Huh?" Stage.**

Something happens, and you're not quite sure how to interpret the whole situation. At this stage, neither of you is too sure if there's a conflict or not. Perhaps your friend said something that you didn't quite hear, or maybe you're not sure how to interpret their comment. It's like trying to read a confusing text message full of emojis from your grandma. The advice that I would give regarding this situation is to approach the person directly:

Approach the person and ask them directly if there genuinely is any conflict brewing between the two of you. Be open and honest, and don't try to beat around the bush. This is a great way to prevent any misunderstandings and keep the situation from bubbling into something that is downright uncontrollable.

Think about your own behavior. We can be so quick to judge other people's behavior, but we don't actually take the time to think about how our actions impact and influence the whole situation. Do you think you might have said something that rubbed them the wrong way? If it does hit you at that moment that, oh, dear, you said something that you maybe shouldn't have—put on your big kid pants and apologize.

Get perspective from a neutral third party. Don't go to a best friend because the natural thing to happen here is they may be tempted or feel obligated to take your side. Maybe there is a colleague who you can trust; ask them for their advice because they may be able to provide you with some insights on how the whole situation can be gauged.

- **Phase 2: The "Oh No, You Didn't!" Stage.**

Emotions are rising high. This is where things start to get a little heated. Your friend made a comment that you don't agree with, or maybe they accidentally spilled their drink on your new shoes. It's like when you're watching your favorite reality TV show, and one of the stars says something shocking; you gasp and blurt out loudly, "Oh no, you didn't!" My advice for when someone says something you don't agree with:

Instead of flying off the handle and shouting at them, you can say something along the lines of: "I see where you're coming from, but I disagree with what you're saying because...." Starting off this way can help you and the other person engage in a much more productive conversation. There may even be a thing or two to learn from them.

Remain respectful. Respect isn't a matter of "I agree with this," it's granting the person freedom to believe in whatever they want without changing their view on things. By remaining respectful, I essentially mean don't be dismissive or use snarky comments (don't let the claws come out).

- **Phase 3: The "I'm Not Backing Down" Stage.**

This is the stage where you're both committed to the conflict and unwilling to back down. Maybe you start bringing up old arguments or throwing shade at each other. It's like a game of tug-of-war, except you're both holding on to your egos instead of a rope. The best strategy I have found when you find yourself in this kind of situation is to back away, especially if the other person is adamant about keeping the whole fight going. Here are some things you can say:

- "I think we should back away from the conversation and come back when we're both feeling a little calmer."
- "I really don't want things to get worse between us. Can we agree to disagree and move on?"
- "I see that we have different opinions, and neither of us is even willing to move past our point of view,

so can we change the topic to something different?"

- **Phase 4: The "Let's Take This Outside" Stage.**

This is the stage where things get physical. Maybe you start pushing or shoving each other, or maybe someone throws a punch. It's like a scene from a cheesy action movie where the hero and the villain finally face off in an epic battle.

- **Phase 5: The "Oops, That Escalated Quickly" Stage.**

Only now do you both realize that maybe you let things go too far. Maybe someone gets hurt, or maybe you both just feel embarrassed. It's like when you accidentally eat too much spicy food, leaving you with a burning sensation in your mouth and a sense of regret in your heart. In these occurrences, the best course of action to take is to apologize. The only problem is that most of us aren't all that good at delivering heartfelt and sincere apologies.

Here are some tips for you to take to heart the next time you want to deliver a heartfelt apology.

   Be intentional with your choice of words. In other words, say the words out loud: "I am sorry. I apologize for letting things get this bad." Words easily get misinterpreted, so being clear, simple, and direct is a way to avoid escalating the situation.

   Take responsibility where you must. "Oh, but if both of us were wrong, why should I be the one to do all the apologizing?" That is something I often hear people say. It's really not about who does or doesn't apologize, but more so about being accountable for and owning up to all the places and parts where we messed up and went wrong.

   Be intentional and direct on how you plan to make things right. For example, if you hurt your friend's feelings by making a harsh and unkind comment, you can add a follow-up statement to the apology that is along the lines of: "I will try to be more considerate in the future about my choice of words, and work on being more compassionate." It's important for the other person to hear these words because it builds that bridge for them to trust you again.

⬤ Make sure the apology is coming from a place of sincerity. People can immediately pick up on it when your apology comes from a place of complacency. As much as possible, put yourself in their shoes, because it will help them grasp the severity of the words you said to them.

IDENTIFYING TENSION

Tension within ourselves can be likened to a bowstring that is being tightly pulled, ready to release its energy toward a target. It arises in potential conflict situations as a natural response to the perceived threat or challenge, much like a bow is drawn to its fullest potential in preparation for the shot. The tension can be uncomfortable, even painful at times, but it serves a crucial purpose in allowing us to respond effectively to the situation at hand.

Just as a skilled archer must learn to control the tension in the bowstring to achieve the desired outcome, we, too, must learn to manage the tension within ourselves. When we can maintain a sense of calm amidst the tension, we are better equipped to make clear-headed decisions and respond with intention rather than react impulsively.

However, just as a bowstring left taut for too long may lose its elasticity, prolonged tension within ourselves can lead to stress and burnout. It is important to recognize when the tension has served its purpose and release it healthily, whether through physical exercise, meditation, or seeking support from loved ones.

But in the end, tension within ourselves is a natural and necessary aspect of navigating conflicts and challenges in life. We can become more resilient and effective in achieving our goals when we learn to harness its power and release it when appropriate.

Identifying Tension Within Yourself

We need to learn how to recognize the signs of tension and find ways to release it before it overtakes us. And the first step to doing that is to understand the variety of ways through which it can show up.

Pay attention to your physical state of being. Tension in the body can manifest itself in a variety of ways. It is often subtle, but incredibly powerful, and grips our bodies like the claws of a predator waiting to pounce. It often starts in our shoulders as a tightness that slowly slithers its way down to our spine, coiling around our muscles like a serpent. When we hold our breaths, we feel it in our chest as the muscles constrict, making it difficult for us to take deep, calming breaths.

Our hands become clammy too, our fingers clenched so tightly that they numb, while our stomach churns with anxiety.

Pressure builds in our temples, and our jaw is locked in place as our teeth gnash together in frustration. The tension spreads, like wildfire burning through our bodies, until our every move becomes a struggle, our every thought consumed by the stress. We often try to shake it off, to loosen the grip it has over us, but it is relentless and it refuses to let go. It seeps into our bones, creating an ache that we can't seem to shake, and it drags us down. It's also a sensation that can become incredibly over-whelming, so much so until it reaches a point where it feels suffocating, as though we are trapped in a tight space, needing to break free. It takes a toll on our bodies, draining our energy and leaving us feeling exhausted and depleted. It's no wonder that tension is known to be the silent killer, slowly eroding our health and well-being.

Monitor your thoughts and emotions: Tension can also be reflected in those. For example, you may notice that you are feeling anxious or irritable, or that you are having repetitive negative thoughts. Let's say you just had a conversation with a friend or a potential colleague, and you're not quite sure how to gauge their reaction or are worried about how to approach them because they said something that simply did not sit right with you. Here are some thoughts that might show up:

- *I feel like I'm not being heard or understood in this situation.*
- *I don't want to give in, but I also don't want to make things worse.*
- *I'm worried that speaking up will make the other person defensive and angry.*
- *This situation is making me feel so tense and anxious.*

- *I don't want to hurt anyone's feelings, but I also don't want to compromise on my beliefs.*
- *What if I'm wrong about this situation and make things worse?*
- *I wish I could just avoid this situation and not have to deal with it.*
- *I don't want this situation to affect my relationships with others.*

Notice your behavior patterns: Tension can impact your behavior, such as making you avoid certain situations or people, or become defensive or argumentative. By reflecting on your behavior patterns, you can notice when tension influences your actions.

Practice mindfulness: Mindfulness techniques such as meditation or deep breathing can help you become more aware of your internal state and identify tension when it arises. Regularly practicing mindfulness can develop a greater sense of self-awareness and teach you to manage tension more effectively.

Let's say you're in a meeting with a colleague who often disagrees with your ideas. As the conversation progresses, you notice that your breathing becomes shallow and your hands start to sweat. You may also notice that you're feeling defensive and on edge. By tuning into these physical sensations, thoughts, and emotions, you can recognize that tension is present and take steps to manage it, such as taking a deep breath or reminding yourself to stay open-minded and focused on the conversation.

Quick Tips for Dealing With Tension

- **Take a step back and assess the situation.**

Conflict can be like a storm brewing on the horizon. When you see the clouds gathering, it's important to take a step back and assess the situation before the storm hits. Just like you would prepare for a storm by securing loose objects and finding shelter, you can prepare for conflict by taking a deep breath and gathering your thoughts. This will help you approach the situation with a clear head and you'll be better able to navigate the tension.

- **Listen actively and seek to understand:**

Conflict, sometimes unnecessarily, becomes tangled because we let it get that bad. It then becomes difficult to unravel and make sense of, but active listening is what can help. As you would carefully unwind a ball of yarn, you can carefully listen to the other person and try to understand their perspective. This means putting aside your own opinions and biases and truly trying to see things from their point of view. By doing so, you may find common ground and be able to start resolving the conflict.

- **Find common ground and work toward a solution.**

Conflict can be like a puzzle with missing pieces. It can be frustrating and difficult to solve, but finding common ground can help fill in the missing pieces. Just like you would work with others to solve a puzzle, you can work with the other person to find common ground and start working toward a solution. This may mean compromising or finding a middle ground, which can help resolve the conflict and move things forward.

- **Take care of yourself and practice self-care.**

Conflict can be like a marathon. It can be physically and emotionally draining, but caring for yourself can help you keep going. Just like drinking water and taking breaks during a marathon, you should take care of yourself during a conflict. This means practicing self-care activities like exercise, meditation, or spending time with loved ones. By taking care of yourself, you'll be better equipped to handle the tension and stress of conflict.

Ho'oponopono

A long time ago, in the lush green valleys of Hawaii, there lived a family. The family had been living in peace for generations until one day, a misunderstanding between two members of the family led to a bitter feud that threatened to tear the family apart. The family elders knew that something had to be done to heal the wounds and restore harmony. They called for a meeting of the family members and introduced them to a practice called *Ho'oponopono*.

Ho'oponopono is a Hawaiian practice used to resolve conflicts and restore harmony. Translated directly, it means "to make right" or "to put things in order."

The family members sat in a circle and began the Ho'oponopono ceremony. They started by acknowledging their mistakes and apologizing to one another. Each person took a turn to share their feelings and express their grievances. As they spoke, tears flowed, and emotions ran high. Then, the family members began a process of forgiveness and reconciliation. They took turns to ask for forgiveness and to forgive each other. They hugged and cried, and slowly the wounds began to heal.

As they continued with the ceremony, they also expressed their gratitude for the blessings they had in their lives and their love for one another. The ceremony ended with a prayer of thanks and a commitment to continue to work on their relationships and keep the peace. The family members left the ceremony feeling lighter and happier. The anger and bitterness that had been tearing them apart had been replaced with love and forgiveness. They knew they had a lot of work to do to keep their relationships strong, but they also knew they had the tools to do it.

Taking Responsibility

There's a lot that I have learned in this lifetime and throughout my career, but the most important things that I would say I've come to learn about responsibility are:

- **We are the captains of our ships.** Don't surrender responsibility for your life. If we want to get anywhere in life, we have to be willing to acknowledge our shortcomings.

- **Honesty is always the best policy.** I love that quote by Brené Brown (2010) from *The Gifts of Imperfection* that goes like this: "Courage is about showing up and letting ourselves be seen. I believe that when we take responsibility, that is what we do." We are allowing people to see that we are human and imperfect, but we're also acknowledging that it is not something we should be ashamed of. When we can hold ourselves accountable, we show people that we value integrity and that we can most certainly be trusted.
- **It's an opportunity to empower ourselves with knowledge.** When we choose to take responsibility, we essentially encourage ourselves to see things from a different light and perspective. And that is certainly not a bad thing because the more curious we are willing to be, the more we will be able to show up with empathy in those moments when we need to do so the most.

Ho'oponopono emphasizes taking responsibility for our own actions and their consequences. It teaches us to acknowledge our mistakes and shortcomings and to seek forgiveness from those we have wronged. By owning up to our mistakes, we can create a safe space for others to express their feelings and concerns. We can apply this in our interactions by being accountable for our words and actions, and by showing empathy and understanding toward others.

Seeking Forgiveness

Forgiveness is a hard thing to do, but in that same breath, it is also such a powerful tool for healing and reconciliation.

Ho'oponopono encourages seeking forgiveness from others and offering forgiveness to those who have wronged us. Forgiveness can help us release negative emotions and move forward with a renewed sense of peace and understanding. In our interactions with others, we can practice forgiveness by letting go of grudges and resentments and by offering forgiveness to those who have hurt us. Some additional things that I also want you to keep in mind about forgiveness are:

- It's not about pretending that what happened didn't happen. Most of us assume that when we choose to forgive someone, it automatically means that we have to forget about what happened. It's not about that. It's simply about ensuring that our hearts do not become bitter because of what happened, because when we are able to release and free our hearts from that anger and that pain, we are able to make changes to our behavior, both for us and the people who hurt us.
- Forgiveness does not mean that your feelings are not valid. You are allowed to be angry, sad, or whatever it is that you are feeling, but you should not allow the feelings to control everything you do.
- Forgiveness does not have to happen over a short period. It's a process, and it takes time. You must be patient with yourself as you work through the process; what matters most is that you are trying.
- Forgiveness is not about denying where we went wrong. It's a dangerous and downright irresponsible thing to do to blame other people for our own shortcomings. When we work on the journey of

forgiveness, we have also to acknowledge the fact that we may need forgiveness from them too.

Maintaining Harmony

Ho'oponopono is all about restoring harmony in relationships and communities. It teaches us to listen to others with an open heart and to communicate respectfully and compassionately. By valuing the opinions and feelings of others, we can create a sense of unity and cooperation. In our interactions with people, we can maintain harmony by practicing and engaging in these behaviors.

Share and express "thank you" like it is free candy. I don't think many of us realize how powerful the words are. "Thank you" are two small words that communicate to the people around us that we see them, appreciate them, and value what they bring to the table. So, take time out of your day to say "thank you" to people for the small and big things that they do; say "thank you" when they offer to bring you your coffee or when they hold the door open for you.

Notice the little things that people do. Recognition is such a big part of helping us maintain harmony in our relationships. Let's say you've picked up on something that a colleague or a friend does really well. Highlight it and point it out. It's going to make them feel good about themselves. Additionally, if you have a partner who often does small things like leave you an "Enjoy your day" or "I appreciate you" messages, take time to show your appreciation. It will go a long way!

Avoid gossiping or talking behind people's backs. Gossip taints and tarnishes harmony, and it's also the quickest way to break the trust that we've worked so hard to build. If someone comes up to you and starts talking about someone, you can respond by saying something like: "I would rather not comment or be a part of this conversation if we're going to be talking about other people."

Offer to help others where you can. Take a hands-on approach and jump in to help wherever and whenever possible. In that same way, people will also be encouraged or willing to help you when you're a little stuck. Also, when you're at home and you see your partner, instead of just assuming that "they've got it handled," ask them, "Are you okay, or is there anything I can do to help you or to make the load a lot easier for you?"

Make sure that you establish boundaries with people so they know what you are willing and not willing to tolerate. Boundaries are about honesty with ourselves and those around us. We cannot build harmony when the relationships with those around us are disrespectful, dysfunctional, and chaotic. People need to know where they stand with us, and we too need to know where we stand with them; that is what will enable us to deal with the ever-changing shifts that come with relationship dynamics.

3

HEAL THE CONFLICTS WITHIN

"The internal war that you wage with yourself, may not necessarily be seen by others, but you always feel it."

— LORRAINE NOLAN

A couple of years ago, I worked with a client, who we will call Mary. Mary had always been a people-pleaser. She would go to great lengths to avoid confrontation and keep everyone around her happy. But one day, she found herself in a situation where she had to choose between her happiness and the expectations of others.

What happened was that she had been offered a job at a company she had always dreamed of working for. The only problem was that the job required her to move across the country, away from her family and friends. She was devastated and torn between her desire to take the job and her fear of disappointing her loved ones.

She spent days agonizing over the decision, feeling trapped by her own conflicting desires. She couldn't sleep, couldn't eat, and couldn't focus on anything else. It felt like her mind was in a constant state of chaos. Finally, after a while, Mary realized that the only way to resolve the internal conflict that was brewing was to listen to her own voice. She took a deep breath, gathered her courage, and decided to take the job. Was it an easy choice for her to make? No, it wasn't, but it was the right one for her. She learned that navigating internal conflict requires honesty, self-awareness, and willingness to take risks. By trusting herself, Mary discovered a newfound sense of confidence and inner peace. She knew that no matter the challenges, she had the strength to face them with grace and courage.

None of us are strangers to internal conflict. We've all had to deal with it. If I had to describe it somehow, I would liken it to a game of tug-of-war between two opposing forces within ourselves. It's the feeling of being torn between two or more choices or desires, each with its own set of benefits and drawbacks.

Imagine yourself standing at a fork in the road, deciding which path to take. One path leads you to a familiar destination, while the other leads to a new and exciting opportunity. You're torn between your desire for the comfort of the familiar and the thrill of the unknown. Each path has its own set of risks and rewards, and you're struggling to decide.

Or in another situation, the internal conflict would bubble up when you're trying to decide whether to speak up or stay quiet in a situation that's important to you. Maybe you're in a meeting with your boss, and you have a great idea, but you're afraid of being rejected, criticized, or even shut down. But on the other hand, you know that if you don't speak up, you'll feel like you missed an opportunity to contribute and make a difference.

In all the examples I have mentioned, the internal conflict shows the struggle between competing desires or values. It can be an incredibly challenging thing to navigate, but by examining your own thoughts and feelings and weighing the pros and cons of each option, you can make decisions that feel true to yourself, decisions that are in alignment with the values that you uphold.

TYPES OF INTERNAL CONFLICT

Internal conflict types are as diverse as they come, and to be able to navigate through them successfully, we have to understand what they are and where they come from. We're going to be spending some time taking a look at all the different kinds and how they impact and influence us.

Moral Conflict

Moral conflict is like a game between your conscience and your desires. It's the feeling of being torn between what you know is right and what you really want to do. It's a tricky situation that we all face at some point.

Imagine you're at a fancy restaurant with your friends, and you notice the waiter has accidentally given you an extra $50 bill with your change. You know that the right thing to do is to return the money to the waiter, but you can't help but think about all the things you could buy with that extra cash. You're torn between your moral compass and your desire for extra spending money.

Moral conflict can also arise in relationships when you're faced with a decision that could potentially hurt someone you care about. For example, you may be tempted to lie to your partner to avoid conflict, but you know that honesty is the best policy. You're torn between your desire to keep the peace and your commitment to truthfulness and respect.

As we look at these scenarios, we can see that moral conflict is a struggle between doing what's right and doing what's easy or desirable. It can be challenging to navigate, but by listening to your conscience, weighing the pros and cons, and considering the impact of your actions on others, you can make a decision that aligns with your values and helps you feel good about yourself. Here are some more practical tips that you can apply in these kinds of situations:

- **Outline the pros and cons for yourself.**

Logic might tell us that the fewest cons would be the best route to follow, but no matter what, working through and making a list for yourself may bring to light a couple of important factors that will help you make a decision. For example, you know that a friend has been stealing supplies from work and you confront them, but they decide to completely ignore you and continue doing what they were doing. The dilemma that you would be faced with here is whether to report them or just keep quiet about it and assume the company can actually afford the loss.

- **Talk it out.**

Discussing the issue with someone you trust can be helpful. They may provide a different perspective on the issue and offer insights that may help you make a decision. Another thing about involving a third party is that they are objective throughout the whole situation, so they won't feel compelled to side with a person simply because you are friends and there's some sort of friendship code that you guys must adhere to.

- **Consider the long-term consequences.**

Reflect on the impact of your actions on your colleagues, your organization, and yourself. Imagine how would you feel if people had to be laid off from their jobs because the company suffered too great a loss due to the missing supplies. Would you be okay with knowing there was something you could've done to stop it? Ask yourself over and over again if the actions you are considering are aligned with your personal values and whether you would be comfortable defending them if they were made public.

- **Seek outside guidance.**

Seeking advice from an impartial party, such as a mentor or a therapist, can give you a fresh perspective and help you clarify your values and goals. In life, we will be faced with situations where we have to make really tough and hard decisions, and that is why it's important for us to be certain about what we are, and are not, willing to stand for.

Sexual Conflict

Janice is a child of a single teenage mother who struggled to raise her three children. Early in life, Janice promised herself she would go to college and be financially secure before she had children. With this in mind, she got on birth control and required her boyfriend to use a condom. In her third year of college, Janice met a young man who swept her off her feet. They had similar dreams, goals, and interests. A year into their committed relationship, Mark expressed interest in stopping hormonal birth control and relying solely on the condom. He was concerned about the possible side effects it could have on Janice's health.

This sexual conflict can also be described as the psychological tension or ambivalence wfe experience when our sexual desires or interests conflict with our goals, values, or beliefs. It literally is a battle between the heart and the mind.

On one side of the battlefield, we have the heart, which represents our emotional and physical desires. The heart may be driven by a variety of factors, such as attraction, lust, or love.

When we experience sexual desire, our hearts may be filled with passion, excitement, and longing. We may feel a strong urge to pursue our desires, even if it means taking risks or going against our better judgment.

On the other side of the battlefield, we have the mind, which represents our rational and ethical considerations. The reason may be guided by various factors, such as social norms, personal values, or moral principles. When we face a sexual dilemma, our minds may be filled with doubt, guilt, or confusion. We may feel torn between our desire for pleasure and our sense of responsibility or self-respect.

The result of this battle is a complex and often conflicted inner landscape where our desires and our values are constantly at odds. Sometimes our hearts may win, and we may give in to our sexual impulses, even if it means betraying our principles or putting ourselves at risk. Other times, our minds may prevail, and we may resist our sexual urges, even if it means denying ourselves pleasure or intimacy.

It's ultimately a struggle between our primal instincts and our higher ideals. It is a battle that we all must face at some point in our lives as we navigate the complex terrain of human sexuality. By reconciling our desires and values, we can achieve a greater sense of balance and harmony in our sexual lives. Let's see how it is that we can achieve that.

- **You have to get honest with yourself and your partner.**

Establishing healthy sexual boundaries will require you to become comfortable having uncomfortable conversations about sexuality, and all the areas and factors that sometimes lead you to stray from your values. Look into things or situations where you think you may need to learn to stop yourself or enforce stronger boundaries.

- **Remind yourself over and over again that your boundaries are valid.**

I think that often in relationships, we tend to want to accommodate our partners more than we're willing to accommodate ourselves. We put aside all that we want in order to see them happy, and as a result, we loosen the grip a little on the boundaries that we set for ourselves. But this way of doing things puts us in truly compromising situations. You are allowed to be vocal about your needs, what you want, and what you do not want.

- **Surround yourself with empowering people.**

The kind of people we surround ourselves with has a very strong effect on how much we are actually willing to commit to sticking to our own boundaries. If you surround yourself with people who respect the decisions you make, you're going to feel a lot more empowered to stick around and stay true to your boundaries. For instance, if you are choosing to abstain, but surround yourself with the kind of people who ridicule you for your choices, then there's a part of you that will eventually start to ask, *What's the whole point of upholding these boundaries?*

- **Remind yourself of the "whys" behind your sexual choices.**

The reasons behind our "why" give us the willpower we need to keep holding on when it all seems way too hard and pointless. Think about all of those reasons, why they matter to you, and how you felt when you made those choices.

Self-Image Conflict

Do you ever just tell yourself you're going to start working harder than before to make your dreams a reality, but your behaviors and state of thinking say a completely other thing? That's self-image conflict.

Internal self-image conflict is that disconnect that we feel when our self-concept or self-esteem conflicts with our actual behavior or circumstances. One way to understand internal self-image conflict is to think of it as a tug-of-war between two opposing forces. On one side of the rope, our ideal self represents our aspirations and goals. Our ideal self is the person we want to be, the image we have of ourselves at our best. We may have high expectations for ourselves, such as being successful, competent, or likable. We may feel inspired, motivated, and confident when we think of our ideal selves.

On the other side of the rope, we have our actual self, which represents our current behavior and circumstances. Our actual self is the person we are right now, with all our flaws, weaknesses, and limitations. We may have made mistakes or failed to meet our own expectations. When we compare our actual self to our ideal self, we may feel disappointed, frustrated, or ashamed.

The result of this tug-of-war is a complex and often painful inner conflict in which our aspirations and our reality are constantly at odds. Sometimes our ideal selves may win, and we may strive to improve ourselves, even if it means pushing ourselves out of our comfort zone. Other times, our actual selves may prevail, and we may give in to our weaknesses or make excuses for our behavior, even if it means betraying our ideals.

Ultimately, internal self-image conflict is a struggle between who we want to be and who we are. It is a battle that we all must face at some point in our lives as we navigate the complex terrain of personal growth and self-acceptance. By understanding our own internal conflicts and finding ways to reconcile our ideal selves with our actual selves, we can achieve a greater sense of harmony and authenticity in our lives. Here are a few more things that I want you to remember:

- **You have to know what your core values and beliefs are.**

Our core values are like the anchors that hold our ships steady in a stormy sea. Without them, we would be tossed and turned in every direction, uncertain of which way to go. In the same way, our core values provide us with a sense of direction and purpose in life. They keep us grounded and focused on what truly matters, even when the winds of change and challenges blow against us. As long as we stay true to our core values, we can weather any storm and navigate our way to success and fulfillment. When you know and are aware of your values and beliefs in your heart of hearts, you will be able to work toward aligning your thoughts and actions with them.

- **Self-awareness is a game-changer.**

Take time to reflect on your thoughts and feelings. Observe your self-talk and identify any patterns of negative self-talk or beliefs that are contributing to the conflict. Self-awareness allows you to recognize and acknowledge areas of conflict, which is a critical first step toward addressing them.

- **Fight against that negative self-talk.**

What we say and what we believe about ourselves can have a significant impact on our self-image. When you notice negative thoughts or beliefs, challenge them by asking yourself if they are valid. If they are not, replace them with affirmative statements that are truth-filled and aligned with who you are.

- **Find the support you need.**

Sometimes a little guidance is all that we need, and talking to someone else will help us see things in a different light and get out of our heads a little. Be it a friend or a family member, it doesn't matter. There may be something valuable for you to take from the wisdom they offer.

Existential Conflict

It's a lot like having a debate with yourself about the meaning of life. Having two tiny versions of yourself sitting on your shoulders, one representing your logical side and the other your emotional side, arguing back and forth about what the heck you're doing with your existence. It's a tug-of-war between your head and your heart, with your brain shouting, "You need to be productive and make a difference in the world!" while your heart screams, "But what's the point if it doesn't make you happy?"

Imagine you're a superhero, deciding whether to save the world or take a day off to binge-watch your favorite TV show. The superhero part of you feels like you should be out there doing good, but the lazy part of you just wants to veg out and forget about the world's problems for a while. Or maybe it's like being a plant that's torn between growing toward the sun or growing toward the shade. Your logical side tells you to go toward the light and be productive, while your emotional side tells you to take a break and rest in the shade for a bit.

It's a battle between your responsibilities and your desires, your ambitions, and your self-care. And sometimes, it feels like both sides are equally matched, leaving you in indecision and confusion. But you don't have to worry, because as frustrating and as exhausting as this conflict is, it's an entirely normal part of being human. You don't have to have all the answers in one go; that's where most of the joy of being alive comes from!

- **Embrace the absurdity.**

When you're feeling lost in the meaninglessness of existence, try to find the humor in it all. After all, what's more absurd than a bunch of hairless apes wandering around on a rock hurtling through space? So, laugh at the ridiculousness of it all, and don't take yourself too seriously.

- **Indulge in guilty pleasures.**

Sometimes, the best way to deal with a crisis of meaning is to just indulge in something that makes you happy. So go ahead and binge-watch that trashy reality show or eat that entire carton of ice cream. You might not save the world, but at least you'll enjoy yourself.

- **Connect with others.**

When you're feeling lost, connecting with others who are going through similar struggles can be helpful. Join a support group or find a community online. You may not find all the answers, but at least you'll know you're not alone in your confusion.

- **Find meaning in the meaningless.**

Sometimes, the most profound meaning can be found in the most meaningless things. Take a walk in nature, watch the clouds go by, or stare at a wall and contemplate the absurdity of it all. You may not find any concrete answers, but you could find peace in the contemplation, and that, I believe, is a rather remarkable thing to experience.

THE EMOTIONAL IMPACT OF CONFLICT

Our emotions are the biggest giveaway that a certain need has or hasn't been met. And in most cases, when there is a specific need that has or hasn't been met, those emotions can lead to inner conflict, and sometimes also translate into conflict with those people we love and value the most.

Anger

I want to start with a story about a man named John. John was charismatic, but he also had a terrible temper and is abusive. Whenever anything went wrong in his life, he would explode in a fit of anger, lashing out at whoever was nearby. One day, his wife, Sarah, accidentally spilled gravy on his shirt. Instead of calmly handling the situation, he immediately flew into a rage. He yelled at her, calling her names and blaming her for his ruined shirt.

Sarah was hurt and confused by John's words and irrational outbursts. She didn't understand why he was so angry over something like a gravy stain. Over time, John's frequent outbursts of anger began to take a toll on their relationship. Sarah started to feel like she was walking on eggshells around him, afraid to say or do anything that might set him off.

The problem was that John didn't know how to manage his anger. Instead of taking a deep breath and trying to calm down, he let his emotions take over. This made him feel angry and resentful all the time, even when there was no reason to be upset. As a result, his internal anger began to spill over into his relationships with the people he cared about most. His friends and family started to avoid him, not wanting to deal with his unpredictable and explosive temper.

He eventually realized that his anger was hurting the people he loved. So, he took it upon himself to start exploring the possible places where his anger might have come from. It wasn't an easy thing to do, but over time, this understanding of where the anger came from helped him make amends with the people he had hurt in the past.

This behavior is abusive and unacceptable and it isn't any one's responsibility to manage another person's issues.

Anger is a natural human emotion that can arise because of various factors; it's complex in the sense that it varies from person to person. Sometimes it arises when our egos feel threatened—that could be in the form of our personal status or individual safety. For example, if you're driving and another driver cuts right in front of you, endangering your immediate safety, you may feel an immediate sense of anger wash over you because this careless person has just threatened your personal safety. Or alternatively, if there's a presentation that you've been working on for ages and a manager or coworker dismisses your efforts and tells you it's not up to par, your ego may feel bruised because this person is refusing to recognize how much effort you put into this project.

It comes from frustration, too, like why your partner won't ever put the toilet seat down—like it's that hard of a thing to do. When feeling disrespected—how could that lady at Starbucks offer unsolicited weight loss advice? We experience it when we feel that a great injustice has been done against us. Some people may have a genetic predisposition toward anger and may have difficulty regulating their emotions. In contrast, others may learn it from their environment, such as family dynamics or societal factors.

Allowing ourselves the space to appropriately express our anger, to understand it, is about making space for the thing that was not allowed—our needs, our voice. Allow yourself to:

- **Understand what it is.** Anger stems from those moments when we feel something is off. When our anger is not heard, when it's denied, survival energy starts to build up within us, and over time, that leads to various layers of tension, defensiveness, and urgency.
- **Don't just work on releasing it.** Release without repair and reconnection will not lead to any sustainable change. Working with and not against your anger is about acknowledging its role in your life, not about ignoring it or running away from yourself. Acknowledge, don't deny the validity of its existence.
- **Learn as much as you can from it.** Part of what our anger wants to do is protect us. What needs protection within your system? Is it your truth, your identity, your

voice, your boundaries? When you do find the answer to that question, proceed and ask yourself what needs to be done to fulfill that. That is how you make progress.

Resentment

Resentment is a powerful emotion that can consume us if we let it. It happens in all sorts of relationships, such as parent-child relationships, friendships, working relationships as well as romantic relationships. At its core, it stems from frustration, disempowerment, and sometimes also a sense of feeling stuck. Some other factors that contribute to resentment in relationships are:

- Feeling like there is no space for you. You're constantly putting the other person before you.
- Feeling that you aren't able to express yourself or show up as vulnerably as you can.
- Unrealistic expectations of what the other person should be able or willing to do for you.
- Emotional dumping (them sharing their feelings without asking you if you're in the right emotional space).
- A refusal to take accountability for their actions. Not apologizing or avoiding.
- A lack of appreciation for what you do.

It's essential to learn how to address it so that we don't end up causing damage to our relationships with the people we value most. Recognizing that resentment exists is not the greatest feeling in the world, but putting in the work, regardless of how hard or uncomfortable it is for us, can help us with the necessary attitude adjustments and make the change that we need to make.

- **Approach it from a place of curiosity.** Being curious can look like you asking: Where does this come from? Is there anything else that I can do? Are there any other options? Have I voiced the needs that aren't being met?
- **Identify how you may have contributed to the issue at hand.** Sometimes, without even realizing it, we contribute to situations we are resentful about. For example, not asking for help when we need it.
- **Assess whether your expectations are realistic.** Ensure that you're not setting yourself up for resentment if what you need or are asking for isn't reasonable.
- **Express what it is that you need.** What can the other person do to reduce your feelings of being angry, overwhelmed, or frustrated? Tell them: "I would appreciate it if you started doing more of X, Y, and Z…" It's all about attempting to solve the problem together.
- **Make room for the change that you need.** Follow-up conversations are necessary because they allow the changes to occur and come into effect. The person's effort can be quick but does not require perfection. It simply isn't realistic.

Tough conversations will never be easy to have. And that's okay. But we must find it within ourselves to brave through that momentary discomfort to have healthy and thriving relationships with those we love and value most.

Keen Disappointment

Disappointment is like a storm cloud that rolls in on a sunny day. At first, everything seems fine and dandy, but then the sky darkens and the rain starts to pour down. You feel let down, like you were expecting a beautiful day but instead got hit with a downpour. When we experience disappointment, it can create internal conflict. We may feel conflicted about our expectations versus reality, or about our abilities and what we can accomplish. It's like a tug-of-war between what we hoped for and what happened.

It is a tough pill to swallow, but it doesn't have to define us or our worth. By acknowledging our feelings and working through the internal conflict, we can become stronger and more resilient on the other side. Here's some advice to help you work through it:

- **Acknowledge your disappointment.**

It's important to remember that disappointment is a natural part of life. It's okay to feel disappointed, and it's important to acknowledge and work through those feelings. Instead of beating yourself up, try to reframe the situation and focus on what you can learn from it. Maybe you can identify areas for improvement in your training, or maybe you can shift your mindset to focus on the progress you've made rather than on the outcome.

- **Talk about it.**

Pain heals when we release it in spaces and around people who are safe for us. So, instead of shutting yourself off from the rest of the world, talk to your friends and your family and let them know how all of this is affecting you. Alternatively, if you don't feel like talking to anyone, you could channel the disappointment into something like writing or another creative outlet. The whole purpose of "letting it all out" is to give yourself as much room as you need to regulate your emotions.

- **Internal validation.**

No one knows your heart as well as you do, but the thing about disappointment is, it has this tendency to make us feel like we don't know ourselves as well as we thought we did. Remembering your whys and ultimately reminding yourself of the person you are outside of your achievements will help you get back up again after setbacks and disappointments.

FINDING YOUR TRIGGERS

Our triggers are a sign something is amiss, that there is a part of us that feels neglected and that something desperately needs to be addressed. They can be compared to the delicate strings of a musical instrument, waiting to be plucked by the fingers of life's unpredictability. They lay dormant until a moment arises when the tension becomes too great, and then they unleash a symphony of emotions and reactions. Like hidden landmines, they wait for the unsuspecting victim to stumble upon them, igniting a chain reaction that alters the course of their thoughts, feelings, and behaviors. Our triggers are the invisible puppet masters of our lives, pulling the strings that make us dance to their tune, whether we realize it or not, and we need to explore where they come from because understanding them will help us to navigate the conflict situations that may arise in our lives.

TIPS ON HANDLING AND MANAGING OUR TRIGGERS

Managing our triggers helps us to effectively deal with conflict situations in our lives. It's important to know which wounds need to be addressed. This knowledge will allow us to effectively process our pain and heal.

- **Breathe.** There is freedom in doing so. When you feel an emotional trigger coming on, take a deep breath. Close your eyes, inhale deeply through your nose, hold for a few seconds, and then exhale slowly through your mouth. Repeat this process until you feel calmer.
- **Name it.** Try to identify what triggered your emotional response. Is it a person, situation, or thought? Once you identify the trigger, you can begin to address it.
- **Challenge your thoughts.** Our emotions are often triggered by our thoughts. Challenge any negative or irrational thoughts that are fueling your emotional

response. Ask yourself if your thoughts are based on facts or assumptions.

- **Approach yourself from a place of self-compassion.** Be kind and gentle with yourself. Acknowledge that it's okay to feel emotions and it's natural to be triggered at times. Treat yourself with the same kindness and compassion you would offer to a good friend.
- **Engage in self-care.** It will do wonders for you. Take care of yourself physically and emotionally. Get enough sleep, eat healthily, exercise, and engage in activities that bring you joy and relaxation.
- **Practice mindfulness.** When you feel triggered, try to stay present in the moment. Observe your thoughts and emotions without judgment.

ADDRESSING OVERTHINKING

All my overthinkers, where are you?

To those who understand what a struggle and pain it is to deal with overthinking, I'm sure you'd agree it is like trying to untangle a ball of yarn by pulling on every strand. The more you pull, the more tangled it becomes and the harder it is to solve. Instead of helping us find a solution, it makes situations or decision-making more complex and confusing for us.

It's also a lot like Jenga, where you keep adding blocks on top of each other without considering the stability of the tower, but the more blocks you add, the more unstable the tower becomes until it eventually falls apart. Overthinking a problem can add unnecessary layers of complexity that can make the solution more unstable.

And finally, it's also like trying to solve a puzzle with too many missing pieces. You spend so much time focusing on the missing pieces that you forget to work with what you have. Similarly, overthinking a problem can prevent you from using the resources and information you do have to find a solution.

In all of these scenarios, we can see how unproductive it is when you are looking for a solution. It merely creates more confusion, adds unnecessary complexity, and prevents you from working with what you have. Instead, this is what we can do:

- **Create awareness around your tendency to overthink situations.**

Whenever you find yourself debating with yourself about situations, take a step back and STOP thinking. Make a decision.

- **Don't allow your fear to focus on all the things that can go wrong.**

Let's say you've been debating whether you should approach your manager about a problem that's been sitting on your heart for a while. Instead of thinking of the worst-case scenarios (they'll blow up in a fit of rage and sabotage your job), focus on the possible positive outcome; they may appreciate the fact that you approached them to talk about the issue, and on the plus side as well, you're going to feel a lot more at ease about the whole situation!

- **Perspective matters.**

It's easy to blow things out of proportion or make them seem bigger than they are; if you're unsure, simply go ahead and ask someone their opinion of the whole situation.

- **Accept that you can't control the future or what other people's reactions will be.**

Spending so much time worrying about that only takes away from the peace and joy that you can experience right now, so instead, choose to focus and put all your attention into what you can contribute to changing the whole situation, such as speaking up if something is amiss, and playing your part in standing up for yourself.

AREN'T YOU SICK OF PEOPLE LOOKING AT YOU AS IF YOU ARE JUST ANOTHER ANGRY WOMAN?

"Whenever you're in conflict with someone, there is one factor that can make the difference between damaging your relationship and deepening it. That factor is attitude."

— WILLIAM JAMES

As we are growing up, it's common to be taught that conflict is bad and that it only leads to intense negative emotions such as anger, even rage. Because of this, at the first sign of any conflict, we run the other way, suppressing it or covering it with a splash of toxic positivity— "It could be worse!".

Experience tells us this is not the solution. You know an unresolved argument with your partner, coworker, or even child will rear its ugly head at some point in the future. We have an unhealthy relationship with conflict itself.

Imagine that there are no good or bad conflicts and there are no negative emotions. It's only our reactions to the situation that can doom the experience. Conflict can make us stronger, help us to develop empathy, and strengthen relationships but only when we know how to turn a tense problem into a healthy conflict.

Despite advances in equality, there is no denying that certain stereotypes make conflicts harder for women to deal with. In many cases, women will have to deal with more conflicts than men due to their problem-solving nature. Other times, we are left to deal with the conflicts because we are women and it's in our nature. Truth be told, with so many responsibilities and so much stress, our natural ability to resolve conflicts is tested to all limits.

As much as conflict resolution is more challenging for women, it is also something that brings about incredible changes once mastered. Even just understanding your own triggers and how these impact the phases of conflict can be enough to notice positive effects in all of your relationships. It's a breath of fresh air!

Now imagine your ever-improving conflict resolution could be shared with the people in your life who are also dedicated to advancing their skills! That's pushing it a little bit, right? Not necessarily!

People need to know that there are simple yet effective solutions to conflict resolution and they need to hear this from 'real people'. This is where you can make a difference with a quick Amazon review.

You know yourself that reading opinions from those who have tried and tested any product is the most beneficial and you would be amazed at how valuable people find your opinion. In order to create a world with better conflict resolution, we need your reviews.

SCAN THE QR CODE

PART II

RESOLVING THE CONFLICT

4

HEARING WHAT WAS SAID AND WHAT WAS LEFT UNSAID

"We cannot know whether the conflict is bad unless we know who is fighting, why they are fighting, and how they are fighting."

— JONATHAN MARKS

Have you ever had a conversation with someone but felt like something important was left unsaid? Maybe it was a feeling you couldn't quite articulate or a need that you assumed the other person would understand without you saying it aloud. Whatever the case may be, these unspoken words can often lead to misunderstandings and conflicts.

Let me give you an example. Imagine you're in a relationship with someone you really care about. You're both busy with work and other obligations, so you don't get to see each other as much as you'd like. One day, you find out that your partner has planned to go out with some friends on a night you hoped to spend together. You feel disappointed, but you don't say anything, assuming that your partner will realize how much you were looking forward to spending time together and cancel their plans. But instead, your partner goes out with their friends, leaving you feeling hurt and neglected.

In this situation, the words that were left unsaid were the feelings of disappointment and the need for quality time together. Not voicing these needs clearly allowed a conflict to arise between the two of you.

On the other hand, when we do communicate our needs clearly, it can lead to more positive outcomes. For example, imagine that you're working on a group project with some colleagues. You have a specific idea in mind about how to approach the project, but you're not sure if your colleagues will agree with you. Rather than assuming that they'll understand what you want, you express your ideas clearly and explain why you think they'll be effective. Your colleagues listen to your ideas and agree to try them out, resulting in a successful project.

The unsaid words are just as important as those that were said, because they have the power to be the making or breaking points of our conversations. That is why it's so important to not rely on our assumptions or expectations of people.

ARK METHOD TO UNDERSTANDING WHY PEOPLE
GET OFFENDED

Behind all of our behaviors are feelings; beneath our feelings is a need. Beyond that need is a longing—to belong, to feel safe, seen, heard, and recognized as *you*. People thrive in relationships and spaces where they feel seen; it's a universal and unifying experience for us all. A gift in itself that can help us navigate the complexity of human relationships.

The Need to Be Acknowledged

Meet Sarah, a creative who worked at a small marketing agency. A while ago, Sarah worked on a project for weeks, pouring her heart and soul into every little detail. When she finally completed the task, she eagerly sent it off to her boss, all giddy and excited about his feedback.

Days went by, and Sarah heard nothing. She started to feel anxious and unsure about the quality of her work. *Did her boss hate it? Was it not good enough?* She began to doubt herself and her abilities.

Finally, Sarah's boss sent her an email with some minor suggestions for improvement. She felt relieved that her work was not completely rejected but also a bit disappointed. She had hoped for some recognition after all the hard work and effort she had put into the project.

The following day, Sarah's boss announced in a team meeting that the project had been a huge success, and everyone had done a great job. But Sarah, despite the great news, felt no sense of accomplishment or pride. She felt overlooked and undervalued, leaving her feeling demotivated and unappreciated.

Sarah's story teaches us that when we receive an acknowledgment, it makes us feel seen, heard, and valued. It boosts our confidence and motivates us to continue to show up to do our best work. On the other hand, when we're not acknowledged, it leads to feelings of self-doubt, disappointment, and even resentment.

So, what are the psychological reasons why people get offended when they aren't acknowledged? Firstly, acknowledgment is a basic human need. We all want to feel seen and valued by others. When we don't receive an acknowledgment, it can make us feel invisible and unimportant. I often tell people that it is essential to make sure that we tell people often what they mean to us and how much we value their presence in our lives. I think sometimes it's so much easier to focus on people's flaws, especially if we grew up in environments where criticism was encouraged a lot more than praise. One thing I used to have a habit of doing was whenever someone used to annoy me, I would start to create an even bigger scenario in my head to validate that frustration. But something changed when I turned feedback-giving into something much more regular. The structure that I followed was this: I would tell them all the things about them that I was grateful for, and then I would let them know if there were any things that we could work on.

This meant that when I was annoyed with them, I wouldn't only focus on that one thing that they had done wrong; I could also focus on all the other things they had done right. That allowed me to start seeing people as a "whole" rather than that one tiny flaw. Like, "Yes, you do this thing that annoys the living daylights out of me, but then on the other hand, you also do X, which I truly love and appreciate about you."

Secondly, acknowledgement is a form of validation. When someone acknowledges our efforts or accomplishments, or even our presence, it validates that we have something meaningful and valuable to contribute. Without that validation, we may start to question whether our efforts are worthwhile.

Finally, when we're not acknowledged, it can feel like a form of rejection. We put ourselves out there and work hard, and when we don't receive an acknowledgment, it can feel like our efforts were for nothing. The thing about rejection is that it is like falling off a high cliff onto sharp rocks below. When you take a risk, you climb higher and higher up the cliff. You feel the adrenaline pumping through you as you get closer to the edge. You have so much hope that you'll succeed and fly instead of fall. But then, suddenly, you slip and plummet to the ground. The sharp rocks cut into your skin, and the pain is unbearable. You feel like you've hit rock bottom. It's hard to climb back up and try again after that fall. And in a sense, that makes us resent the people who don't give us the acknowledgment we want, and we end up walking around carrying a whole lot of anger in our hearts.

Respect

These are the things that I have learned about respect over my lifetime:

- It's a huge part of knowing our self-worth and what healthy relationships are supposed to be like; it's about knowing what treatment we should accept from others and, in turn, extending the same behavior to those around us.
- It's about accepting people for who they are and what they stand for, even if we don't necessarily agree with their views.
- Respect is like the foundation of a building. A strong foundation is needed for a building to stand tall and withstand any external forces, and respect is essential for any relationship to thrive and withstand challenges. Without respect, a relationship is like a building built on sand—it may appear stable at first, but it's bound to crumble under pressure.
- Respect is such a fundamental aspect of human interaction because it acknowledges the inherent worth and dignity of each individual. When we show respect to others, we recognize their autonomy, beliefs, and values. It's a way of demonstrating that we acknowledge and value their identity and contributions. When we don't show respect, whether intentionally or unintentionally, we are essentially telling the other person that we don't value them as a human being. Unsurprisingly, people get offended

when they don't receive respect. Being disrespected can be hurtful and can damage relationships.

- Let's say you're in a meeting at work, and someone interrupts you while you're speaking. They may not have intended to be disrespectful, but by interrupting you, they're essentially saying that what you have to say isn't important. This can be frustrating and lead to feelings of resentment. On the other hand, if someone listens to you attentively, asks for your opinion, and acknowledges your contributions, it shows that they respect you and value your input.

- Respect is crucial for healthy and successful human interactions. It's a way of acknowledging each individual's worth and dignity and helps build strong and lasting relationships. When we don't receive respect, it can be hurtful and damaging and can lead to conflict and misunderstandings.

The Need to Know Things

Sometimes, we think it's our "right" to know stuff. We feel like people should tell us things because we're acquainted with them or because we're interested in the topic. It's like we have a curiosity itch that needs to be scratched. And when we're left out of the loop, we feel like we're missing out on something important. It's like being the last one picked for a team in gym class or not being invited to a party. It can make us feel left out, unimportant, and even disrespected.

On top of that, we humans are naturally social creatures. We have a desire to connect with others and be part of a community. When someone doesn't tell us something, it can feel like they intentionally excluded us from that community. They're saying, "You're not one of us." This can be hurtful and can cause us to feel angry or resentful toward the person who didn't tell us.

But why do we feel this way? Well, it's because knowledge is power. Knowing things can give us an advantage in various situations, whether it's in our personal or professional lives. It can help us make informed decisions, avoid dangers, and feel more confident. So, when we're not given access to information, it can feel like we're being held back or disadvantaged in some way.

Let's just say that you work in a team with a few other colleagues, and you're all responsible for a project that's due in a couple of weeks. You've been working hard on your part of the project but you notice that one of your colleagues, John, has been working on something you're not aware of. You ask John about it, but he brushes it off and says that it's not important.

A few days later, you find out that John has been working on a crucial part of the project that directly affects your work. You're upset and frustrated because you feel like John should have told you about this earlier. You could have saved time and effort if you had known about it from the beginning.

You start to feel like John intentionally kept this information from you, and you begin to hold a grudge. You start to distance yourself from John and don't include him in important conversations or decisions, which causes tension within the team.

In this example, John's failure to communicate and share information caused you to feel excluded and left out. You felt like you were at a disadvantage because you didn't have access to all the relevant information. This led to a breakdown in trust and communication within the team, which ultimately affected the success of the project.

It's important to remember that in the workplace, communication is key. Keeping information to yourself or failing to communicate effectively can cause misunderstandings and hurt feelings. By being open and transparent with your colleagues, you can build trust, foster collaboration, and ultimately achieve success as a team. In addition, humans have a natural curiosity and desire to connect with others. We feel like it's our right to know things, especially if it's relevant to us. When we're left out of the loop, it can be hurtful and make us feel excluded. Knowledge is power, and not having access to it can make us feel like we're at a disadvantage.

LISTENING

If you have ever played a game of tennis with someone who hits the ball back to you without paying attention to where you're standing on the court, you may know how frustrating that is. You keep hitting the ball to different corners of the court, but your opponent just keeps hitting it back to you without any strategy or thought. Well, that's certainly what it's like when someone only listens to respond in a conversation. They're so focused on hitting the ball back to you (i.e., responding) that they don't pay attention to where you're standing on the court (i.e., your perspective and what you're trying to convey). As a result, the conversation becomes a game of "back-and-forth" without any real understanding or communication taking place.

Just like in tennis, effective communication requires both players to be aware of each other's positions and to work together to move the conversation forward. So, here is a question that I would like you to think about: Do you listen to others to truly understand what they are saying, or are you simply listening so that you can answer?

Now, I don't know about you, but listening is so hard for me sometimes! I mean, have you ever found yourself just nodding along to a conversation, only to realize that you have no idea what the other person is actually saying? And to make matters worse, the person goes on to ask you a question, and you find yourself thinking to yourself at that moment: *Oh, boy, I'm screwed!* If so, you're not alone. Listening is a skill that many of us struggle with, and several obstacles get in our way:

- **Distractions:**

There is certainly no shortage of distractions around us in this day and age. We've got all this technology and social media platforms to compete with. Have you ever tried to have a conversation with someone while the TV or music was blaring in the background? It makes it incredibly difficult to actually focus on what the person is saying. And if you're anything like me, you might even find yourself singing along with the lyrics.

- **Emotions:**

Have you ever been so angry or upset that you couldn't listen to reason? Well, here's the thing; sometimes, our emotions are like a rowdy group of friends at a party. They're loud, they're distracting, and they're definitely not interested in listening to anyone else. So, when we're feeling emotional, it's like our friends are shouting in our ears and we can't focus on anything else. It's hard to really listen when your emotions are screaming "Woohoo!" in your brain the whole time.

- **Bias:**

Well, humans are just like cats. Do you know how cats will only approach people they like and completely ignore those they don't? We do the same thing with our biases. We only really listen to those we already like and tend to tune out those who don't fit within our biased preferences. Our brain is saying, *Sorry, can't hear you; you're not my cup of tea.* Maybe if we start petting people's heads like we do with cats, we'll be more willing to listen to them regardless of biases... or maybe not.

How to Start Active Listening

Active listening is a pretty simple concept to understand—it's all about presence in our conversations. Listening to understand, not simply to respond. It's about taking time to reflect on what the person has said, not rushing, and being intentional in the words that you choose to use. The good news about listening is that it is actually a skill you can improve. I'm not saying you're going to perfect it simply by reading a five-step guide; I'm just saying that with consistency and choosing to make it non-negotiable in your daily interactions, you may just get pretty good at it. Here's how:

- **Allow the person to speak.**

You can do this simply by using eye contact. Maintaining eye contact with someone speaking is a powerful way to show interest in what they're saying. Oh, but remember, you don't want to come across as creepy with your eyes.

- **Use nonverbal cues.**

You want to show them that you are actually listening to them. Nodding your head or giving affirmative gestures, making sure that your posture is open and inviting, smiling at them every now and then, or a thumbs up can also convey that you're following along and understanding the speaker.

- **Practice mirroring.**

Sometimes our personal biases and assumptions distort what we hear. As the listener in a conversation, your main role is to understand what is being said. This is going to require reflection from your side. Paraphrasing or summarizing what the other person has said can demonstrate that you're actively listening and trying to comprehend their message. These can be helpful:

- "So, what I am hearing is this," "Am I correct in saying that…"
- Ask them questions if there are things that you want them to highlight or clarify further. "What do you mean when you say…"

- **Hold judgments.**

Wait for the person to finish speaking completely before you even consider putting in your two cents. If you interrupt them mid-sentence, it limits and creates a barrier to you getting the full message.

- **Eliminate distractions.**

Nothing says "I am not listening to you" like someone who is texting or doing something while you're trying to relay a message to them. If you're easily distracted, make sure to eliminate any potential distractions before the conversation begins. That means turning off your phone, finding a quiet location, and not multitasking!

- **Focus on the message.**

Engage with the message being conveyed instead of just the words. Listen with a curious and open mind rather than just tuning in to specific keywords or phrases. Active listening calls us to approach conversations from a place of compassion and respect. Most of the time, in conversations, especially when it is with people who we are meeting for the very first time, we're getting new information. We learn nothing if we attack the person without clearly understanding what they're saying. If you know that you're someone with strong opinions, be honest but still maintain a respectful note and, most importantly, treat the other person in the same way that you would like to be treated.

Remember that active listening takes practice, so don't get discouraged if you don't feel like a pro at first. With time and patience, you'll be able to hone your active listening skills and become a more effective communicator.

Hearing What Was Unsaid

So, you know how sometimes when we talk to people, they might not say everything they think or feel out loud? Maybe they're trying to be polite, or maybe they don't want to hurt our feelings. Well, the concept of hearing what was unsaid is all about being able to pick up on those unspoken cues and understand what someone is really trying to communicate.

It's kind of like a superpower! By paying attention to things like body language, tone of voice, and even the words that someone chooses to use, we can start to get a sense of what they're really thinking or feeling. And when we can do that, we can have more meaningful and productive conversations with the people in our lives.

Of course, it's not always easy to hear what was unsaid. Sometimes we may misinterpret things or jump to conclusions. But with practice and a bit of intuition, we can improve over time. There are also a few things that you can do, and I can definitely confirm they've worked well for me:

- **Listen for nonverbal cues.**

People communicate more through their body language than through their words. Pay attention to things like facial expressions, posture, and tone of voice to get a better sense of what someone is really trying to convey. For example, if someone speaks in a monotone voice and avoids eye contact, they may feel anxious or uncomfortable or autistic.

- **Ask open-ended questions.**

Instead of asking yes or no questions, ask questions encouraging the other person to share more about their thoughts and feelings. For example, instead of asking, "Do you like your job?" you could ask, "What do you enjoy most about your job?" This can help you better understand the other person's perspective and feelings.

- **Practice active listening.**

When you're having a conversation, try to really focus on what the other person is saying and avoid distractions like your phone or other people around you. Repeat what the other person said in your own words to ensure you've understood correctly. This can also help encourage the other person to share more. For example, if someone says, "I'm really stressed about work," you could respond with, "It sounds like you're feeling overwhelmed with your workload. Can you tell me more about what's been going on?"

Communication is a two-way street, so it's important for us to find and continue working on ways to nurture these relationships and work on communication in a way that allows them to thrive continually.

Social Cues

Reading social cues is an absolute "must know" skill for navigating the complex world of human interactions. Whether you're trying to make a new friend, impress a boss, or simply avoid a social faux pas, being able to pick up on subtle cues can make all the difference.

Sadly though, social cues can be complicated to read at times. It's like trying to decipher a secret code, but it changes every time you think you've cracked it. To make matters worse, people are often not very direct in their communication, leading to confusion and misinterpretation.

For example, have you ever been in a situation where someone said, "I'm fine," but you could tell from their tone of voice and body language that they were anything but fine? Or have you ever tried to make a joke only to have it fall flat because you misread the social context? It can be awkward and uncomfortable.

But fear not! There are ways to improve your social cue reading skills. One of the most important things is to pay attention to nonverbal cues, like facial expressions, body language, and tone of voice. Another key is to practice empathy and try to put yourself in the other person's shoes. What might they be thinking or feeling? Social cues will vary across cultures, so take time to be aware of them.

Ultimately, being able to read social cues is like having a superpower. It can help you connect with others, avoid misunderstandings, and easily navigate social situations. If that's something that you've never learned how to read, I've got you! Here are a few:

- **It's important to understand when someone might want to leave.**

Have you ever been in a situation where you want to leave, but the other person just won't stop talking? Yeah, that's pretty awkward. Usually, when someone wants to leave, they will start looking at their watch or even gear their attention more toward the door.

- **Gauge their interest in the conversation.**

The easiest way to tell if someone wants to continue to talk to you is if they ask you questions and take an actual interest in what you are saying. The more detailed the responses, the bigger the likelihood that they are enjoying the conversation.

- **Notice when they want to change the subject.**

When someone is uncomfortable talking about something and wants to change the subject, you should notice they may want to divert attention away from themselves by asking questions such as "Well, what about you…" Their face might also harden to tell you that "I want to stop this convo right now."

- **Notice when they feel uncomfortable.**

Can you actually tell when you're making someone uncomfortable? Here are some telltale signs:

- They may furrow their eyebrows or purse their lips.
- They may close their body language by crossing their arms.
- They may laugh nervously.
- They may excessively start touching their face or using their arms too much.

Silence Is Not Always Uncomfortable

Have you ever found yourself in a situation with someone where neither of you were saying anything, but it was neither uncomfortable nor awkward? It just felt all right—felt like home? Perhaps you were watching a sunset or a sunrise with a friend or enjoying a scenic walk. In these moments, silence can be especially comforting and peaceful.

A lot of us fear silence because we think that when we're with people, we automatically have to be exchanging words, but that's not the case. Sometimes, we need that silence to recharge our social batteries and to connect with our thoughts and our emotions fully. It's like getting a break from all the noise out there and getting back in touch with yourself. So, the next time you find yourself in an eerily silent moment, embrace and enjoy it. It may be exactly what you need. Here's how you can learn to be okay with silence in conversations:

- **Understand the purpose of the silence.** Perhaps you and the other person just need a moment or two to think about what was said. You need those moments to think about an appropriate response.
- **Understand that in most cases and situations, people actually appreciate those moments of silence.** Not everyone wants to be talking the whole time, so if you and the person you're communicating with can actually share a moment or two of silence, they'll appreciate you for that.
- **It makes conversations more meaningful.** Intentionality is highly attractive. Take time to think about what you want to say and don't speak just because you want to fill in gaps.

5

IN THE THICK OF THINGS

Have you ever been embroiled in a heated workplace argument over something seemingly trivial, like a misplaced stapler or a missed deadline? Despite their small size, these seemingly inconsequential issues can quickly snowball into full-blown conflicts, derailing productivity and damaging relationships. Studies have shown that workplace conflict can cost companies billions of dollars each year. But why do these petty grievances have such a potent effect on our emotions and our working relationships? We will explore the hidden dynamics of workplace conflict and uncover strategies for resolving even the smallest of issues.

In Chapters 1 and 2, we went into detail about conflict in the workplace, and we also discussed the different types of internal conflict. In this section, we're going to spend a bit of time working on trying to understand intergroup and interorganizational conflict.

INTERGROUP CONFLICT

So, let's just imagine we're at a potluck dinner that we've been looking forward to for weeks now, and everyone will be bringing their favorite dish to share. And somewhere in between conversations, two people started arguing over which dish was better. One of them insisted that their lasagna was the best thing to happen to the world since sliced bread, while the other person insisted that their mac and cheese dish was quite literally God's gift to the universe. This argument started to escalate quite quickly, and soon, other people at the potluck started taking sides. Some people sided with the lasagna person, while others sided with the mac and cheese person. Eventually, the argument became so heated that the potluck was no longer enjoyable for anyone.

When we're in the workplace, intergroup conflict can start similarly. It often begins with a disagreement or difference of opinion between two groups within the company. This disagreement then escalates into a full-blown conflict if people start taking sides and emotions run high. Let's say your company just landed a big new client, and there are two teams within the company that have different approaches to completing a project. One team believes a more conservative approach would work best, while the other team believes a more aggressive approach is necessary. As the teams work together, tensions start to rise and people begin to take sides. Eventually, the conflict becomes so intense that it starts to affect the productivity and morale of the entire company.

In both the potluck and workplace scenarios, we can see that the intergroup conflict started off with a small disagreement that blew up into something bigger. The key to preventing this from happening is to address any disagreements or differences of opinion early on, before they have a chance to escalate. By encouraging open communication and collaboration, people can work together to find a solution that works for everyone rather than getting bogged down in an intergroup conflict.

INTERORGANIZATIONAL CONFLICT

Imagine you were captain of a ship navigating across the sea, and you came across another ship heading in the opposite direction, and as your ships passed each other, there was a brief exchange of words between your crews. You might have noticed that your crew became increasingly agitated.

Upon further investigation, you discovered that the other ship was actually a rival ship that was competing with your ship for the same cargo. That would mean the crews of both ships are in a state of interorganizational conflict. In our usual workplace environments, interorganizational conflict can often start similarly. It typically begins when your company and a competitor compete for the same clients, contracts, or resources. This can lead to tension and hostility between the companies, which can escalate into a full-blown corporate war if not managed properly.

Unlike intergroup conflict within a single organization, interorganizational conflict involves conflict between different organizations. Interorganizational conflict can be more complex and difficult to manage, as it involves multiple stakeholders with different goals and objectives.

Another example is two companies bidding for the same contract with a third company. As the bidding process unfolds, tensions start to rise between the two companies, with each trying to outdo the other. This can lead to aggressive tactics, such as spreading negative rumors or undercutting prices, further escalating the conflict.

The key to preventing this conflict from escalating is to establish clear lines of communication and set realistic expectations and boundaries. Both organizations can avoid a damaging and costly conflict by finding common ground and working toward a mutually beneficial solution.

IT'S NOT ABOUT WINNING

Conflict resolution is not a competition. It's not about who gets the first word in and who gets the last word. What would it be like to live in a world where every disagreement or conflict was solved through competition? It would be a never-ending cycle of winners and losers, with no real resolution or growth. Instead of working together to find a solution, we would perpetually be pitted against each other in a battle for supremacy. This type of mentality not only hinders progress but can also lead to bitterness and resentment. When we are solely focused on winning, we lose sight of the bigger picture and the potential for collaboration.

In reality, true success is not measured by who wins, but by the ability to work together toward a common goal. When we embrace cooperation and empathy, our conflicts can be resolved in a way that benefits everyone involved.

Let's create a scenario where you and a friend try to decide where to go for dinner. You suggest your favorite Italian restaurant, but they're not in the mood for Italian food and suggest a Mexican restaurant instead. You both feel strongly about your choice of restaurant and start to argue, each of you trying to convince the other that your choice is better. However, instead of continuing to argue and compete with each other, you both decide to take a step back and consider the situation from each other's perspective. You realize that your friend may not be in the mood for Italian food because that's what they had for lunch, and your friend realizes that you are really craving Italian food. So, eventually, you decide to try a new restaurant that serves a fusion of Italian and Mexican cuisine, which satisfies both of your preferences. This is a win-win situation, where both of you are able to get what you want without having to compete or compromise too much.

Creating a win-win situation in the workplace requires a similar approach. Instead of trying to win the conflict at all costs, everybody needs to consider the perspectives of those involved and work together to find a solution that benefits everyone. This can be through brainstorming creative solutions, compromising on certain aspects of the conflict, or finding common ground that allows both parties to achieve their goals.

Imagine a company is considering a major restructuring project that will affect multiple departments, and one department is concerned the restructuring will result in job losses. In contrast, another department is excited about the opportunity for growth and development. Instead of competing with each other or trying to win the battle, both departments can work together to find a solution that benefits everyone. This could involve reassigning employees to different roles, creating new positions within the company, or providing training and development opportunities for employees who may be affected by the restructuring.

When we focus on everyone's needs and interests, we create a space that allows everyone to come out ahead. Instead of seeing conflict as a competition, it becomes an opportunity for collaboration and growth.

Us Versus the Problem

The "us versus the problem" mindset is a powerful and productive approach to conflict resolution in our relationships. It recognizes that the problem is the enemy, not the people involved in the conflict—because that is ultimately how most of us approach conflict situations, we end up perceiving the person on the other end as the enemy, rather than the problem. Shifting our focus away from blaming and attacking each other and toward working together to solve the problem, promotes a more collaborative and constructive approach to conflict resolution.

We tend to become defensive, explosive, and reactive when approaching conflict with a "problem versus us" mindset. We may feel threatened—that's why our natural response is to defend ourselves and our position. This can quickly escalate the conflict and make it more difficult to find a resolution.

On the other hand, when we approach conflict with an "us versus the problem" mindset, we are often more open to hearing each other's perspectives and working together to find a solution. We can focus on understanding the problem and finding a solution that works for both parties, rather than trying to win the argument or prove that we are right.

I love it when people kiss and make up; I love reconciliation. Conflict should never really be about who comes out on top. It's all about unity, rebuilding the trust and relationship we once had with that person. It's about learning to put our egos aside and preserving a special place for peace in our relationships.

Here are some tips on what you can do to develop an "us versus the problem" attitude toward conflict:

- **Make the problem the center of attention, not the person:** When addressing a conflict, it's important to focus on the problem and not place blame on the other person. This helps to reduce defensiveness and encourages a collaborative approach to finding a solution.
- **Meet each other halfway; that means finding common ground.** Even amid a conflict, there may be

areas of agreement or shared interests between you and the other. Identifying this common ground can help you build a foundation for finding a mutually beneficial solution.

- **Brainstorm solutions together:** Rather than imposing your solution on the other person, how about you work together to brainstorm various potential solutions? This will help to promote a sense of collaboration and shared ownership of the solution.

- **Don't let assumptions get in the way:** It's easy to make assumptions about the other person's intentions, character, or motivations during a conflict. However, most of the time, these assumptions are unfounded and inaccurate; this is where the misunderstanding typically happens. So, check your assumptions by asking the other person to clarify their perspective.

MEDIATION

Sometimes, we just need that third party to step in on a situation. And I can definitely help with that!

Think of it this way: Mediation is like having a referee for your arguments, but instead of throwing flags and blowing whistles, they help you find common ground and reach a resolution. It's like having a personal Gandalf to guide you through the dark and treacherous forest of disagreement.

Imagine you and your friend are arguing over who gets to choose the pizza toppings for your next lunch date. You're both getting pretty hot and bothered and soon start to throw insults back and forth at each other. That's where the mediator would come in handy: The wise and impartial third party who listens to your arguments and helps you find a solution that works for both of you. Suddenly, you are no longer enemies, but allies working together to enjoy a delicious pizza topping combination.

The benefits of mediation are numerous. For one, it can help reduce a conflict's emotional intensity by providing an objective perspective and creating a neutral space for communication. It can also help to improve communication skills and promote understanding between parties, leading to stronger and more positive relationships.

Types of Mediation

One of the things I especially love about mediation is that it can be approached in various ways. Yes, it's a serious subject, but that doesn't necessarily mean we can't have fun with it. Here are three types of mediation, with examples of how they can be approached in everyday life.

Facilitative Mediation

I like to think of it like a group project in school. You know, one of those projects where you're assigned to work with a bunch of people you barely know, and you have to somehow come up with a cohesive presentation or report. Facilitative mediation is having a teacher or a tutor who guides the group to work together effectively. The mediator helps the group communicate, stay on task, and come up with a solution that everyone can agree on.

Evaluative Mediation

Imagine yourself in a scenario where you're watching a cooking competition show, and the judges taste the dishes and give feedback on what they think is good or bad about each dish. Evaluative mediation is similar in the sense that the mediator evaluates the strengths and weaknesses of each party's argument and helps them understand the likely outcome if they were to go to court. The mediator acts like the judge on the show, giving feedback and helping the parties come to a resolution.

Transformative Mediation

This one is a lot like the relationship between a gardener and a plant. The gardener tends to the plant, nurturing it and helping it grow. The plant may have some issues, like not enough sunlight, too much water, or pests, but the gardener works with the plant to address those issues and help it thrive. Transformative mediation is similar in that the mediator helps the people involved address the underlying issues that are causing the conflict. The mediator acts like the gardener, helping them grow and transform their relationship into a more positive and productive one.

Tips on Becoming an Excellent Mediator

At some point, you may find yourself in a position where you're tasked with the challenge of being the mediator between feuds, but what is it that makes a good mediator? Well, you're about to find out.

Being a good listener. One of the most important things you can do as a mediator is to be a good listener. Listen to each party's words and try to understand their perspective. Don't interrupt and don't make assumptions. Instead, ask questions to clarify their position.

You have to be able to remain neutral and unbiased. As a mediator, it's crucial to remain neutral. Don't take sides or show favoritism toward one party or the other. Your job is to help the parties come to a resolution that works for everyone, not to pick a winner.

Keep the conversation on track. It's easy for conversations to get derailed when emotions run high. As the mediator, keeping the conversation on track is your job. If the conversation starts to veer off course, gently steer it back to the main issue at hand.

Try to identify areas where the parties have common ground. This can help build trust and create a foundation for a resolution. Look for shared goals or interests and find ways to build on them.

Practice patience. Mediation can be a slow and grueling process, and it's important to be patient. Don't rush the parties to come to a resolution. Instead, give them the time they need to express their concerns and work through the issues fully. Remember, the goal is to find a solution that works for everyone, not to quickly resolve the conflict.

NEGOTIATION AS A MEASURE OF CONFLICT RESOLUTION

The great thing about negotiation is that it allows all of us to have a say in the outcome. It's not about one party winning and the other losing, like a game of Mouse Trap gone wrong. It's about finding that point of equilibrium that works for everyone, like two mice agreeing to share a piece of cheese without getting into a fight.

It can also be particularly useful in conflict resolution because it creates a space where everyone has the stage to express their needs and wants, like two cats negotiating who gets to sleep in the sunny spot by the window. Maybe the one needs the warmth to help with an achy joint, while the other just wants to soak up some rays. By negotiating, they can find a solution that works for both of them, like taking turns in the sun or sharing the space. It also helps us nurture trust and respect, things that can help us create a positive relationship that extends far beyond the specific conflict at hand.

HOW TO NEGOTIATE PROPERLY

Negotiation is a skill, and knowing how to navigate it properly can help you (and the other person) come out at the top! Here are some tips and tricks you can keep up your sleeve.

- **Zip it and listen.** I think there's one thing we've learned throughout the book, which is that sometimes, the very best thing to do is to keep quiet and listen. So many conflicts that erupt can be saved in this way.

- **Don't be afraid of a little pushback.** You will not be able to negotiate effectively if you're unwilling to challenge the validity of what the other person is saying. There is nothing wrong with a bit of challenge, but you also need to keep in mind that there is a very big difference between challenge and disrespect.
- **You have to be willing to understand when it's time to walk away.** Sometimes negotiations don't go as planned, and if there is somewhere where you're not willing to draw the line, you might find yourself caving in to the other person's demands.
- **Show how the other person will benefit as well.** Successful negotiations are all about the win-win element for everyone involved. So, before going into the negotiation, make sure that you map and plan out how you intend to satisfy the other person's needs.
- **Don't worry too much about things you cannot control; these are things such as the other person's personality.** Negotiations often fail because we spend too much time obsessing over these things and taking them personally and to heart. So, if someone is rude or difficult to deal with, it's not on you but more on them; remember that.

6

THE VALUE OF DIVERSITY

Diversity is a garden, and just like any garden is made more beautiful by the variety of plants and flowers it houses, our thoughts and actions are enriched through the diversity of people we interact with. Everyone brings with them a unique set of perspectives, experiences, and knowledge that can broaden our understanding of the world.

But, like any garden, diversity in our relationships can sometimes be the birthplace of conflict in our relationships. Just like how certain plants clash with each other or compete for resources to thrive, our different beliefs, values, and experiences may clash and create tension in our relationships. For example, suppose you and a coworker come from different cultural backgrounds. In that case, you both may have different approaches to teamwork or communication, and if neither of you understands the dynamic of the other, it will end up leading to misunderstandings or disagreements. Let's take a look at some types of conflict that can arise due to diversity.

- **Communication conflict.**

Communication styles differ from culture to culture. This conflict may arise when people from different cultural backgrounds have different communication styles and struggle to understand each other. For example, a team member from a high-context culture, such as Japan, may communicate more indirectly, while a team member from a low-context culture, such as the United States, may prefer more direct communication.

- **Values conflict.**

We weren't all raised in the same way, nor do we all believe the same things. Values conflict happens when individuals have different beliefs or values that clash with each other. For instance, a team member who values work-life balance may have difficulty understanding a coworker who prioritizes working long hours to get ahead.

- **Perception conflict.**

How I interpret something is not necessarily the same way in which you interpret that same thing. Perception conflicts arise when we see the same situation differently because of our unique experiences and biases. For instance, a team member who has experienced discrimination may perceive a comment or action as discriminatory, while another team member may not see it that way.

- **Goal conflict.**

When we have different priorities or objectives while working on projects in the workplace, we may end up having differences with the people who we are working with. For instance, a team member that is mainly focused on meeting a tight deadline may be at odds with a coworker who wants to take a more thorough approach to a project.

We should always keep in mind, however, that these conflicts are not inherently negative because, in most situations, they can often lead to new insights and solutions if handled effectively and in the right way.

INCLUSIVITY AS A SOLUTION TO CONFLICT

Have you ever felt left out or excluded from a group or activity? It can be a pretty terrible feeling, right? That's why inclusivity is so important—it's about making sure that everyone feels welcome and valued, no matter who they are or where they come from. But inclusivity is about more than just being nice to people. It's actually a powerful tool for solving conflict. When we include diverse perspectives and voices, we can come up with more creative solutions to problems. We can also better understand and empathize with people who may have different experiences or opinions than us.

Think about it like this: If you're trying to solve a problem with a group of people who all think the same way, you're probably not going to get very far in that discussion, but if you bring in people with different backgrounds, skills, and viewpoints, you'll have a much better chance of finding a solution that works for everyone. Here are some ways through which you can advocate for and create a more accepting space for everyone at work.

- **Foster empathy.**

Inclusivity requires empathy, or the ability to understand and share the feelings of others. When conflicts arise, it's important to foster empathy by encouraging team members to put themselves in each other's shoes. This can be done through exercises such as role-playing or brainstorming sessions where team members are encouraged to consider multiple perspectives.

- **Promote cultural awareness.**

Inclusive teams are aware of and celebrate the diversity of their members. By promoting cultural awareness, team members can better understand each other's backgrounds and cultural nuances, which can help avoid misunderstandings and conflicts. This can be done through cultural awareness training, team-building exercises, or simply by encouraging team members to share their cultural experiences with each other.

- **Use collaborative problem-solving.**

When conflicts arise, it's essential to approach them as a team rather than as individuals. By using collaborative problem-solving techniques, such as brainstorming or consensus-building, team members can work together to find solutions that work for everyone. This approach resolves conflicts and can improve team cohesion and trust.

- **Create a safe space for feedback.**

When people are in a safe space, the need to be defensive is reduced significantly. Create a safe environment where team members or colleagues can provide feedback to each other without fear of retaliation or judgment. When conflicts arise, team members should feel comfortable providing feedback to each other constructively and respectfully. By creating a culture where feedback is encouraged and valued, communication in the workplace between colleagues will significantly improve.

MANAGING YOUR ANGER

Imagine anger as a wild and powerful horse. When tamed and guided properly, this horse can help us accomplish great things and even take us on thrilling adventures. But if left unchecked, it can bolt out of control and cause chaos and destruction. Learning to manage anger is like learning to ride this powerful horse. It requires patience, practice, and skill. Just as a skilled rider can control the horse's movements and direct it toward its desired destination, managing anger allows us to harness its energy and use it to achieve our goals in a constructive way.

But if we don't learn to manage our anger, it can become overwhelming and dangerous, causing us to lash out and hurt others or ourselves—similar to how an untamed horse would cause harm and destruction to our relationships and our own well-being.

So, just as we must learn to tame and guide a wild horse, we must also learn to manage our anger so that we can harness its power and use it for good.

- **Tip 1:** Give it enough room to breathe. Allow it to take up space and tell you what it is exactly that you're experiencing. Be with it. Bottling it up or pushing it away only increases the risk of it coming up in an uncontrollable burst.
- **Tip 2:** Allow for irrational thoughts to exist. Anger can sometimes create feelings that make us want to get revenge. It causes sadness and pain to build up in our hearts. Don't judge yourself for that. Anger is a normal and even healthy emotion.
- **Tip 3:** Don't make impulsive decisions. Being angry is not an ideal state in which to make rational decisions or have a constructive and meaningful conversation with someone. Give yourself some time to think about your anger and to fully process it.

POLITENESS IS YOUR ALLY

Imagine you are on a journey through a vast and unfamiliar land. Along the way, you encounter all sorts of people—some friendly, some indifferent, and some outright hostile.

Now, imagine that politeness is your trusty traveling companion on this journey. It's like a loyal friend who has your back no matter what. When you are polite to others, you show them that you respect and value them as fellow travelers on the road of life. You create a sense of goodwill and cooperation to help you navigate even the toughest challenges. Just like a skilled navigator who knows how to read the stars and chart a course through choppy waters, politeness helps you navigate the complex social landscape of human interaction. It helps you avoid misunderstandings, defuse tense situations, and build bridges between people with different perspectives or backgrounds.

Remember that politeness is your ally next time you find yourself in a difficult social situation. The compass can guide you through even the most treacherous terrain and help you reach your destination with grace and dignity.

Questions to Ask Yourself

Politeness can really help you go a long way when it comes to conflict resolution. Here are some questions you can ask yourself to approach the conflict situation with more self-awareness, empathy, and gratitude.

- What is the root cause of the conflict I'm about to engage in?
- Have I taken the time to reflect on my emotions and thoughts surrounding this conflict?
- Can I clearly articulate my perspective and feelings on the matter?
- Have I considered the other person's perspective and feelings?
- Am I approaching this conflict with an open mind and a willingness to understand the other person's point of view?
- What is my primary goal in engaging in this conflict, and is it a constructive one?
- Can I communicate my thoughts and feelings without using accusatory language or raising my voice?
- Have I considered the most appropriate time and place to discuss this conflict?
- Am I prepared to listen actively and empathetically to the other person's story?
- Can I identify any potential areas of compromise or common ground that could help resolve the conflict?

THE GREATNESS OF GRATITUDE

Gratitude is good because it turns denial into acceptance, chaos into order, confusion into clarity, problems into opportunities, failures into successes, and enemies into friends.

Now, you might be thinking: What relationship does gratitude have with conflict resolution? Well allow me to explain. When we're in a conflict with someone, it's easier to focus on what they've done wrong, what they should have done differently, and the pain they've caused us. However, dwelling on these negative aspects only leads to a downward spiral of anger, resentment, and mistrust.

On the other hand, when we choose to practice gratitude, it helps us shift our focus to the positive aspects of the situation. It helps us appreciate the other person's strengths, good intentions, and everything they've done right. By doing so, we can start to see the conflict from their perspective and find common ground for resolution.

Gratitude also helps to diffuse negative emotions and promote positive ones, such as empathy, kindness, and forgiveness. When we express gratitude toward someone, we acknowledge their value and worth as a person, which can help us build trust and strengthen the relationship. It's not always easy to choose gratitude—to choose to see the good in all things—but when we do, it makes us better people. So, even when it's hard, I hope that we can choose to be good, to be kind.

Kindness is the glue that binds us together, the salve that heals our wounds, and the light that guides us out of the darkness. It requires us to step outside of ourselves, to see the world from another's perspective, to extend a hand of compassion, and to listen with an open heart. Kindness is not a weakness; rather, it's a strength that requires courage and vulnerability. It's the final step toward conflict resolution because it's the ultimate act of love and forgiveness that allows us to make peace with ourselves and the other person.

In the next chapter, we'll dive into all things related to the peace that comes at the end of conflict resolution. I am excited about that because nothing feels as good as being in harmony with the people around us. Let's jump right into it, shall we?

PART III

BIRTHING PEACE

7

MAKE PEACE

"Eventually, I know that we will all arrive at that place where we realize that prioritizing peace is far more important than being right all the time."

— CARLA HENRY LEWIS

O ur minds are like the water in a pond. When all is calm and still, we can see straight to the bottom and appreciate the beauty of the view below. But when there are ripples and waves, the water becomes murky, and it's hard to see anything clearly.

In the same way, when our minds are calm and at peace, we can see things more clearly and are able to appreciate the beauty of life. We can focus on our goals and dreams and make good decisions that benefit ourselves and those around us. But when we're constantly distracted by stress, anxiety, and negative emotions, our minds become murky, and it's hard to see anything clearly. We may make impulsive decisions that we later regret or get stuck in negative thought patterns that hold us back from reaching our full potential.

That's why inner peace is so important. When we cultivate inner peace through practices like forgiveness, conflict resolution, meditation, mindfulness, or spending time in nature, we can tap into our inner wisdom and make choices that align with our values and goals. We can approach challenges with a clearer state of mind and an open heart, and find creative solutions to problems that might have seemed overwhelming before. Ultimately, cultivating inner peace allows us to live more fulfilling and meaningful lives, and to share our light with the world around us.

ENDING CONFLICT IN A RELATIONSHIP

It's easier to hold a grudge and hold on to anger because anger is the one emotion that affirms that we've been dealt an ugly hand. But you know what's better than holding on to anger? Reconciliation.

Our relationships are such an important part of our inner world. When our relationships are strong and healthy, we feel supported and loved, and our minds are at peace. But when we have unresolved conflicts with the people in our lives, or feel wounded by them, it can create a lot of cluttering emotional "weeds" that make it harder to find peace and happiness.

Just like we need to tend to our garden by pulling out unwanted weeds to keep it healthy, we need to tend to our relationships and work through any conflicts or misunderstandings to keep our inner world at peace. When we take the time to listen to each other, apologize when necessary, and work toward forgiveness, we create a more harmonious inner world that allows us to thrive and grow.

A beautiful garden requires regular maintenance and weeding to stay healthy; like a garden, your heart, too, needs that same maintenance for your emotional well-being.

HOW TO MAINTAIN YOUR PEACE OF MIND

Peace of mind. That elusive state of being where the stresses and worries of daily life melt away like ice cream on a hot summer day. It's something we all crave. Finding it can be a bit like searching for a needle in a haystack, but I know it doesn't have to be that way. Here are a few things that you can consider doing to encourage a calmer state of mind.

- **Get your Zen on.** Peace of mind is cultivated through presence. Whether meditation, yoga, or simply taking a few deep breaths, finding your inner peace can often start with finding your inner calm. Take time each day to focus on your breath and let those worries float away like a leaf on a gentle breeze.
- **Disconnect to reconnect.** In today's hyper-connected world, getting caught up in the endless scroll of social media, email, and notifications can be too easy. Take a

break from your devices and spend some time in nature, reading a book, or enjoying quiet time.

- **Spoil yourself.** Sometimes all it takes to find peace of mind is a little indulgence. Take a bubble bath, splurge on that fancy coffee, or treat yourself to a massage. You deserve it!
- **Get moving.** Exercise is not only good for the body, it's also a great way to clear your mind. Whether it's a brisk walk, a yoga class, or a high-intensity workout, finding a physical activity you enjoy can help you release tension and boost your mood.
- **Practice gratitude:** It's easy to get caught up in the things we don't have or the problems we're facing, but taking a moment each day to focus on the things we're grateful for can help shift our perspective and bring us a sense of peace and contentment.

Ensuring Peace Endures After the Fight

You see, making peace isn't just about ending violence or hostilities. It's about finding a way to coexist with others in a respectful, compassionate, and empathetic way. It's about recognizing the humanity in one another, even when we disagree or have different beliefs.

In conflict resolution, making peace often means finding common ground with someone we may perceive as an adversary. It means listening to their perspective, understanding their needs and fears, and working together to find a solution that benefits both parties. It means letting go of our egos and opinions and being open to the possibility that there may be more than one correct answer.

But making peace goes beyond just the individuals involved in a conflict. It's about creating a culture of peace that values cooperation, understanding, and forgiveness. It's about recognizing that we are all interconnected and that our actions impact the world around us. It's about being willing to take responsibility for our role in a conflict and working toward a solution that benefits everyone, not just ourselves.

Remember, peace is about so much more than ending a war. It's about creating a world where conflict is resolved with empathy, understanding, and a willingness to work together. It's about recognizing that we are all in this together and that together we are better.

Practice forgiveness. Holding on to grudges and resentment only fuels further conflict in the future. When we forgive someone, it's like planting a seed in the garden of our relationships. At first, it may be vulnerable to the weeds of resentment and anger, but with care and attention, that seed can grow into a healthy relationship. Just like a garden must be watered, fertilized, and weeded regularly, forgiveness requires ongoing effort and attention.

But just like a garden, forgiveness can be challenging. It's not always easy to let go of hurt and pain, just as it's not always easy to pull up weeds or repel pests. But with each act of forgiveness, we're nurturing the garden of our relationships and creating a space full of love, compassion, and understanding.

Respect people's choices, boundaries, and needs, even if it's something that you don't particularly understand.

Don't be afraid to compromise. Finding the middle ground and reaching solutions for everyone is essential in helping partners nurture healthy peace.

THERE IS NO POWER STRUGGLE IN CONFLICT RESOLUTION. THE GREATEST POWER LIES WITHIN YOU!

One of the most valuable lessons we learned throughout our life experiences and this collaboration was from a holocaust survivor, Viktor Frankl. We have the power to choose how we react. Faced with aggression, there is a split second when you can fight fire with fire, or you can engage in the powerful skills you have discovered. There is one other split-second decision we need you to make!

WE WANT TO HEAR FROM YOU!
IF YOU ENJOYED THIS BOOK, PLEASE LEAVE A REVIEW TO HELP OTHERS

As authors, we value your opinions. They provide us with a chance to connect with you and create more content that can make a positive impact on your life. More importantly, when you share your opinion on Amazon, others who are fighting conflicts left, right, and center can discover the A.R.K. method as some much-needed peace in their lives.

SCAN THE QR CODE

CONCLUSION

As we go about life, we will encounter various types of conflict that range in magnitude. These clashes are going to mostly be a result of differences in opinions, values, or perspectives. However, when we choose to approach these complex situations in a way that makes people feel acknowledged, we create environments where mutual respect and kindness are at the forefront, and that will certainly have a significant impact on how the whole situation plays out.

Acknowledgment has always been and will always be a fundamental human need. That is something that will never ever change. When we provide acknowledgment, we demonstrate that people matter and that we value and appreciate their presence in our lives. Acknowledgment will always be effective in conflict resolution because it helps everyone feel seen and heard. This is what creates a sense of trust between individuals and allows us to respect each other's perspectives.

And let's not forget kindness, which can create a ripple effect that has the power to extend far beyond the conflict at hand. Treating people with dignity and compassion encourages them to follow suit in their behaviors. Which creates more harmony in our day-to-day interactions with them.

A.R.K. (Acknowledgment, Respect, Know)—make that your everyday mantra and guiding compass when dealing with difficult people. It won't always make conflicts a breeze to navigate, but it does give us the wisdom we need to come out at the other end of our conflicts as better people.

REFERENCES

Abrahams, R., & Groysberg, B. (2021, December 21). *How to become a better listener.* Harvard Business Review. https://hbr.org/2021/12/how-to-become-a-better-listener

Admin. (2023, January 1). *Understanding ho'oponopono: A beautiful hawaiian teaching about forgiveness.* Grace & Lightness. https://graceandlightness.com/hooponopono-for-forgiveness/

Bensla, A. (2023, January 18). *5 common types Of conflicts in the workplace and their causes.* Risely. https://www.risely.me/5-common-types-of-conflicts-in-the-workplace/

Berman, J. (2019, May 1). *The power of wholeness and healing: ho'oponopono.* Compassionate Listen. https://www.compassionatelistening.org/post/power-of-wholeness-and-healing

Bower, T. (2021, January 3). *Gratitude is good: why it's important and how to ultimate It.* Forbes. https://www.forbes.com/sites/tracybrower/2021/01/03/gratitude-is-good-why-its-important-and-how-to-cultivate-it

Brown, B. (2010). *The gifts of imperfection: let go of who you think you're supposed to be and embrace who you are.* Hazelden.

Conflict resolution quotes. QuotesGram. (n.d.). https://quotesgram.com/conflict-resolution-quotes/

DeMarco, M. (2021, August 4). *Being comfortable with silence is a superpower.* Forge. https://forge.medium.com/being-comfortable-with-silence-is-a-superpower-64b9e0e54925

Dixita. (2020, November 3). *5 conflict management styles to improve your productivity.* Matter. https://matterapp.com/blog/5-conflict-management-styles-to-improve-your-productivity

Edmondson, A. (2012, June 6). *The psychology of conflict, and 4 ways to work it out.* Fast Company. https://www.fastcompany.com/1839408/psychology-conflict-and-4-ways-work-it-out

Effective communication is key to resolving conflicts. (n.d.). Army and Navy Academy. https://www.armyandnavyacademy.org/blog/effective-communication-is-key-to-resolving-conflicts/

Expert Panel (2020, June 8). *Council post: 15 critical skills required to become an excel-

lent negotiator. Forbes. https://www.forbes.com/sites/forbescoachescouncil/2020/07/08/15-critical-skills-required-to-become-an-excellent-negotiator

Faoliu, A. (2016, June 17). *Summary of "judgmental biases in conflict resolution and how to overcome them."* Beyond Intractability. https://www.beyondin tractability.org/artsum/thompson-judgmental

Feigenbaum, E. (2010). *Differences and conflict in diversity.* Chron. https://small business.chron.com/differences-conflict-diversity-3045.html

Fearon, E. (2021, March 31). *Shifting the power: The role of women in conflict resolution and peacekeeping.* Human Rights Pulse. https://www.humanright spulse.com/mastercontentblog/shifting-the-power-the-role-of-women-in-conflict-resolution-and-peacekeeping

The five main causes of conflict. Vilendrer Law. https://www.vilendrerlaw.com/five-main-causes-conflict-mediation-can-resolve/

5 types of workplace conflicts & how to resolve them. (2021, April 19). Camelo Blog. https://blog.camelohq.com/5-types-of-workplace-conflicts/

4 ways to communicate during conflict in your relationship. (2021, February 4). Oregon Counseling. https://oregoncounseling.com/article/4-ways-to-communicate-during-conflict-in-your-relationship/

Fresne, A. *Mastering your emotions.* Elevate. https://www.ellevatenetwork.com/articles/9776-mastering-your-emotions

Gunthe, R. (2013, May 31). *Escalating stages of conflict.* Psychology Today. https://www.psychologytoday.com/us/blog/rediscovering-love/201905/escalating-stages-conflict

Ho'oponopono. (n.d.) https://www.laughteronlineuniversity.com/hoopono pono-4-simple-steps/

Holl, E. (2021). *Causes, consequences, and solutions for intergroup conflict.* ADR Times. https://www.adrtimes.com/intergroup-conflict/

Holland, K. (2019, January 29). *How to Control Anger: 25 Tips to Manage Your Anger and Feel Calmer.* Healthline. https://www.healthline.com/health/mental-health/how-to-control-anger#1

Indeed Editorial Team. (n.d.). *7 types of internal conflict in literature (plus how to use them).* Indeed Career Guide. https://www.indeed.com/career-advice/career-development/types-of-internal-conflict

Join One Love. (2016, November 4). *7 tips for handling conflict in your relationship.* One Love Foundation. https://www.joinonelove.org/learn/handling_conflict/

Jones, H. (2021, December 20). *What are social cues?* Verywell Health. https://www.verywellhealth.com/social-cues-5204407

Juneja, P. (2015). *Understanding conflict—Meaning and phases of conflict.* Managementstudyguide.com.https://www.managementstudyguide.com/understanding-conflict.htm

Koh, J. A. (2022, November 18). *Council post: The plum blossom principles: Develop deep strategic listening skills.* Forbes. https://www.forbes.com/sites/forbescoachescouncil/2022/11/18/the-plum-blossom-principles-develop-deep-strategic-listening-skills

Kuligowski, K. (2019a). *4 Communication tips to resolve workplace conflicts.* Business News Daily. https://www.businessnewsdaily.com/8766-resolving-workplace-conflicts.html

Lewandowski, G. W. (2021, June 10). *The 10 most common sources of conflict in relationships.* Psychology Today. https://www.psychologytoday.com/us/blog/the-psychology-relationships/202106/the-10-most-common-sources-conflict-in-relationships

Make peace, not war: five ways to resolve any conflict. (n.d.). NYC Therapist for Anxiety, Depression, & Couples Counseling. https://www.happyapplenyc.com/blog/make-peace-not-war-five-ways-to-resolve-any-conflict

Morin, A. (2021, July 30). *11 ways to calm yourself fast when you're really mad.* Verywell Mind. https://www.verywellmind.com/anger-management-strategies-4178870

Noll, D. (2000, November 17). *Conflict escalation: A five phase model.* Mediate.com. https://mediate.com/conflict-escalation-a-five-phase-model/

Pon Staff. (2023, March 27). *The mediation process and dispute resolution.* PON - Program on Negotiation at Harvard Law School. https://www.pon.harvard.edu/daily/mediation/dispute-resolution-how-mediation-unfolds/

Raypole, C. (2020, April 28). *How to control your emotions: 11 strategies to try.* Healthline. https://www.healthline.com/health/how-to-control-your-emotions

Regan, S. (2021, June 28). *Are you good at reading social cues? See if you recognize these 17 Common Ones.* Mindbodygreen. https://www.mindbodygreen.com/articles/social-cues-types-and-how-to-read-them

Risser, M. (2022, May 24). *Interpersonal conflicts: types, examples & resolution*

Strategies. Choosing Therapy. https://www.choosingtherapy.com/interpersonal-conflicts/

Robbins, T. (2015, April 20). *6 strategic ways to develop emotional mastery.* Tonyrobbins.com. https://www.tonyrobbins.com/mind-meaning/be-the-master-of-your-emotions/

Shonk, K. (2023, March 23). *Negotiation as a means of conflict resolution https://www.pon.harvard.edu/tag/conflict-negotiation/#:*

Typenote. (2021, February 12). *Causes of conflict: 10 reasons of conflict in the Organization.* https://tyonote.com/causes_of_conflict_in_the_organization/

Vestergaard, B., Helvard, E., & Rieck Sørensen, A. (2011). *Conflict resolution—working with conflicts.* https://konfliktloesning.dk/wp-content/uploads/2017/04/ConflictResolution.pdf

Walter, N. (2016, May 23). *Peacemaking.* Beyond Intractability. https://www.beyondintractability.org/coreknowledge/peacemaking

What is conflict sources? (2022) https://study.com/learn/lesson/what-is-conflict-sources-types.html

White, M. (2021, January 1). *Example of interorganizational conflict.* Bizfluent. https://bizfluent.com/example-of-interorganizational-conflict.html

Why is negotiation important in conflict resolution? (n.d.). Ailit. https://ailit.org/why-is-negotiation-important-in-conflict-resolution/

www.ingramcontent.com/pod-product-compliance
Lightning Source LLC
Chambersburg PA
CBHW022057020426
42335CB00012B/730